TACKLE BADMINTON

Tackle Badminton

ROGER J. MILLS
and
ERIC BUTLER

Foreword by
NANCY HORNER

STANLEY PAUL
London

STANLEY PAUL & CO LTD
3 Fitzroy Square, London W1

AN IMPRINT OF THE HUTCHINSON GROUP

London Melbourne Sydney Auckland
Wellington Johannesburg Cape Town
and agencies throughout the world

First published 1966
Second impression January 1969
Revised edition February 1974

© Roger J. Mills and Eric Butler 1966, 1974

Printed in Great Britain by litho on antique wove paper
by Anchor Press, and bound by Wm. Brendon,
both of Tiptree, Essex

ISBN 0 09 119220 X (cased)
     0 09 119221 8 (paper)

To the Badminton enthusiast

Acknowledgements

Educational Productions Ltd., 17 Denbigh Street, London S.W.1 (for the use of photographs).

Notes for Umpires—Badminton Umpires Association of England.

Notes for Badminton Coaches—Badminton Association of England.

Contents

	Foreword	13
	Introduction	17
1	Development of the game	19
2	Start on the right foot	23
3	Get a grip of your game	28
4	Serve it this way: receive it this way	33
5	Stroke it this way	38
	Play it this way—an introduction	47
6	Singles play	49
7	Doubles (men's and ladies')	56
8	Mixed doubles	62
9	Match play	67
10	Watch it this way	74
11	Umpiring and coaching	78
12	Keep fit this way	94
13	Badminton: a world-wide game —the future	100
	Epilogue	105
	Laws of Badminton	106
	Glossary of terms	121
	Recommended reading	124

Illustrations

Roger Mills	*facing page*	36
A well-dressed foursome		36
Preparing for an overhead shot		37
Just before impact		37
Preparing to serve		44
At impact of service		44
Receiving service		44
Preparing for backhand shot		45
At full stretch at point of impact		45
'Round the head' shot		80
Underarm backhand		80
Taking shuttle early at net		81
Attacking a loose drop shot		81
An English Thomas Cup team at Amager Badminton Club, Copenhagen		96
A mixed doubles showing back and front formation on both sides		96
The England team which toured South Africa, Rhodesia, Zambia and South-West Africa in 1965		97
Surrey first team 1965. County champions for the ninth time		97

Foreword

By NANCY HORNER

I commend this book to all badminton players, whether beginners or experienced players, because it contains much sound good sense for everyone. This, of course, is no more than is to be expected from two such authors—Eric Butler, a writer of great experience who has already collaborated in producing a number of books on sport, and Roger Mills, one of England's current international players.

I have known Roger Mills as a badminton player for a long time, because, although he is now only in his middle twenties, he played the game, and showed undoubted promise, at the tender age of eleven. He first won the All-England Junior Singles and Mixed Doubles titles in the 1957-8 season, when only fifteen years old. Now a regular choice for the England team, he excels in all three branches of the game, unlike many an international player of the past and present. In spite of his small stature he is able by speed of foot and a varied repertoire of strokes, coupled with considerable deception, to defeat players possessed of superior height and physical strength.

Roger, however, is not just a born 'natural', as he

has a fine tactical brain, and knows the whys and wherefores of the matches in which he plays. Not all top-grade players in a sport are capable of this analysis. In addition he has a great deal of enthusiasm for the game, which inspires young players around him, and he is always willing to give advice when asked, and to do some coaching where required.

All this adds up to a person who is eminently qualified to advise others on the game of badminton. Being a top-class player, he can discuss the game in all its aspects, technical and tactical. Having travelled abroad as an English international, he is in a position to describe play and players in other countries. By dint of having lent a helping hand in coaching others, he has an understanding of the difficulties of the game even where the less-gifted are concerned. I feel it will not be out of place, too, to mention that of recent years he has been suffering from diabetes, and has managed to overcome the difficulties involved, and to carry on as before with competitive play.

To those of you who have played badminton for some time, there is probably no need for me to detail its attractions, but to those who have only watched the world stars at Wembley, or, indeed, have neither yet played nor seen the game, a few words of explanation are perhaps not out of place. This is a sport which suits the English weather. It needs a high ceiling, it is true, but otherwise a court can be fitted into most reasonable-sized halls. Did you realise that at the National Sports Centre at Lilleshall in Shropshire the main sports hall is marked out for only two tennis courts, but superimposed on this area are the lines for *eight* badminton courts?

Badminton is a delightful game for the beginner, as most people find the shuttlecock easy to strike after a fashion. It is possible to have some sort of rally right from the outset, even if the action takes place on only a small part of the court near the net! Physical strength is not of paramount importance, and so the little girl can take part, and have as enjoyable a game as the big rugby forward. And, speaking of boys and girls, I would stress that mixed doubles at badminton is one of the fastest and most satisfactory games there are, the lady, who normally plays at the net, having an opportunity to use her delicacy of shot while her partner does the heavy work from behind. As the racket is so light, it can be readily wielded even by a small child, which means that we have here a very suitable school game. This fact is obviously being recognised, as recently an English Schools Badminton Association has been formed, due to the large increase in the number of schools playing the game. Changed days from the time when I played at school in Scotland and all we had to play against in matches were the adults of the local church clubs!

In conclusion, I would like to pay a special tribute to the spirit in which badminton is played throughout the world. I have myself met and played against representatives from a variety of countries, and the standard of behaviour on the court and the fine sportsmanship shown generally have always impressed me greatly. International fixtures do an immense amount of good to foster friendly relations with other countries. One such occasion was the 1965 tour of South Africa by an England team, including Roger Mills, when a number of Test matches were played before huge and most appreciative audiences. No doubt the people there and elsewhere who have seen him play will agree with my summing-up of Roger as a great sportsman, a cheery opponent, a pleasant personality and a hard worker.

Introduction

We feel we have achieved what we set out to do—compile a short but complete instruction book on the fundamental playing and administrative principles of badminton, the world and the family game.

There may well have been more detailed books, but we have made an honest attempt to simplify the approach and provide an interesting basis for improvement of the reader's game—indeed an interesting and modern way of 'tackling' badminton.

In writing this book we have aimed at teaching the beginner all the elementary points in what can be a very fascinating game for players of all ages. At the same time, we feel that many advanced club and tournament players will derive some benefit from our labours.

Throughout the book we have used the masculine personal pronoun for men and ladies, except where the subject under review concerns ladies only.

All directions are for right-handed players and should be reversed for 'lefties'.

All instructions are only rule-of-thumb.

I

Development of the game

The game was first named when army officers on leave from India played at Badminton in 1873 on a county estate owned by the Duke of Beaufort in Gloucestershire, England. It appears to have been played at Poona in India a year earlier by English officers, but it also appears that the game was played in both China and Poland in the seventeenth and eighteenth centuries and there are even references in twelfth century English royal court records.

The first really organised body was the English Badminton Association, formed in 1893, and it was England who began touring such countries as Canada and Denmark in the 1920's to foster the game.

Naturally, English emigrants began playing in all the Commonwealth countries, with the result that the International Badminton Federation was founded in London in 1934.

The nine founder member countries have since been joined by forty-one others. Incidentally, there are over 3,500 affiliated clubs in England, and about half a million players.

The democracy of badminton administration is an

epitome of fairness. Every club in England has the opportunity of affiliating to its county association, who, in turn, affiliate to the national body. The Badminton Association of England is governed by a council consisting of elected representatives of all the county associations, plus twelve co-opted members, three of whom are regular tournament players. Two members of this council represent England at I.B.F. meetings. Thus every player can express his opinions through this democratic pyramid and can have a voice in the general management of the game throughout the world. It is not, therefore, accidental that the game has international uniformity with regard to the laws and equipment.

The I.B.F. is governed by an annual meeting of the elected representatives of every national association in membership and before any alteration in the laws of the game can be adopted it must be approved by at least two-thirds of the meeting.

Badminton at present is essentially an amateur sport and, except for a few professional coaches, all badminton players are strictly amateur. Consequently, globe-trotting tours used to be rare occurrences. Only occasionally could a particular championship event ensure large enough attendances to invite top-class players and pay their expenses. Occasionally, however, sponsors for championships can be obtained, and nowadays this is more and more becoming the trend.

Nevertheless, a large number of international matches take place annually and official teams are sent abroad to compete in international tournaments and to foster international relationships.

Although badminton had a somewhat quiet and unannounced initiation at the beginning of the century, its growth—despite being impeded by two world wars—has been steady and efficient. Moreover, since 1946 the game has obviously (and painfully so to English players who have hopes of achieving a world-class standard) gained such enthusiasm in countries such as Malaya, Denmark, Indonesia and Thailand that it is now their No. 1 sport.

Why has badminton become so popular in such a short space of time and what is its appeal compared to other sports?

Above all, the game is domestically ideal; by that one means that all members of the family, immaterial of age or sex, can play and enjoy it because the equipment is light and easy to handle. Its tremendous appeal is mainly due to the unique flight of the shuttlecock. When hit softly it travels slower than any other object in any other sport, but when hit hard and correctly it can travel off the racket at over 100 miles an hour. Because of the particular make-up of the shuttle, the pliable goose feathers fold in at impact, but open out after a split second, causing rapid deceleration. This 'slowing-up' provides the main enjoyment of the game—i.e. long rallies and near impossible returns by the defender.

Naturally, the pace of the game depends on the ability of the players. The beginner will hit the shuttle slowly backwards and forwards, endeavouring merely to get the shuttle over the net, while the skilled player can use the lightness of his equipment to change direction, trajectory and speed of the shuttle; his wrist to delay production of the shot; and his footwork and anticipation to get to the shuttle as early as possible before it hits the floor.

The fact that the game is all volleying makes it one

of the fastest and most exhausting pursuits in the athletic world. Because the player is allowed little time to think he must learn to react quickly and be fit enough to continue doing so for sometimes as long as an hour of continuous play.

Unfortunately, except in certain countries, badminton cannot be played outdoors because of the extreme lightness of the shuttle, which is affected by the slightest breeze. Consequently, most players tend to perform mainly in winter only so that they can take part in other sports during the summer months. In view of the climatic conditions in England in particular the game is becoming increasingly popular, as one is not dependent upon the weather in order to play.

2

Start on the right foot

The racket

There are no official specifications for the weight or size of a racket, but in general it weighs between 5 and 5½ oz. and is about 26 in. long. A heavier racket will provide more power, but this advantage is offset by the subsequent loss of speed in manœuvring. The most important factors in choosing a suitable racket are its balance and grip, both of which should feel comfortable when the user swings it at an imaginary shuttle. The fact that it will be manipulated mainly by the wrist must be remembered. Too thin a handle should be avoided, as this tends to make the player grip the racket too tightly, causing tenseness and often leading to tennis elbow.

The better rackets these days have a steel shaft but are still as flexible as the old wooden shafts. A racket should be kept in an even-pressured press at all times when not in use and care should be taken to keep it away from possible heat or dampness in order to avoid warping.

The gut should be fairly taut, giving a clear high

pitched 'ping' when flicked with the finger. When held up to the light the gut itself should be of clear appearance. Nylon stringing is hard wearing but does not have the same resilience. In 1966, however, revolutionary all-steel rackets were produced weighing less than the wooden ones; they do not require a press, and have become popular world-wide since then.

Shuttlecocks

A shuttle, otherwise known as a bird or feather, is of unique design. It is composed of sixteen goose feathers inserted in a cork base covered by kid, and weighs only a fifth or sixth of an ounce. It is prudent to remember, economically speaking, that one goose equals one good-quality shuttle; therefore great care should be taken to preserve the life of this delicate article. The tubes, specially treated by the manufacturers, should be kept at a cool-moist temperature; any dryness or heat will cause them to break up quickly.

Because of the varying conditions of the weather and the atmosphere in different halls, shuttles are made to fly at various speeds and these are determined by a range of weight from 73 to 85 grains with a small pellet inserted into the cork. Generally speaking, rounded-feathered shuttlecocks are about two grains slower than pointed feathers.

Less expensive synthetic shuttles made of nylon plastic are now officially used in most countries. They cannot yet compare with the delicacy of feathers, but the action and flight are being improved rapidly as the result of research. No.4 in the Laws of Badminton (see page 110) deals with the correct speed and method of testing shuttles.

Clothing

Most tournament organisers insist that all contestants wear white apparel and—despite the heavy laundry bills—we would advise everyone to observe the custom except perhaps for an austere-coloured sweater during practice.

Clothing should fit comfortably, allowing freedom of movement and shot production. It is important to feel smartly dressed, as one will give an appearance of being accomplished and automatically play better.

As the game demands a lot of running, twisting and jerky footwork, one should be careful to choose a strong pair of white, well-cushioned rubber-soled shoes that are light and have a good grip on the court. They should be large enough to fit snugly even when wearing thick woollen socks which prevent the feet becoming sore and blistered.

The court

The size of the whole court is 44 ft. long by 20 ft. wide (for detailed measurements see the diagram (page 108) in Laws of Badminton).

The ideal hall for a badminton court should be 30 ft. in height at the centre, though the higher the better. The background should be uniform in colour, preferably a dull, medium green, and the floor a dark brown wood which is not slippery.

Court lines, $1\frac{1}{2}$ in. wide, should be painted in white, while the best posts to use are those on a metal base screwed into the floor, though posts with guy ropes or weighted bases will be found quite suitable.

Daylight from the roof or the sides of the court is permissible, but any brightness from either end should be entirely blacked out, as the objective is to have the shuttle standing out clearly against a dark background.

Two types of artificial lighting are suitable:

1. Four lamps of about 80 candle power, each hanging about 2 ft. outside each side of the centre of the court and about 12 ft. above it, or

2. One naked light of about 750 candle power at each side of the centre of the court (see diagram).

It is best to have about 3 ft. space around the court.

Basic rules

At this stage it is necessary to clarify certain points in the Laws of Badminton for players in their early stages of the game.

Only the side *serving* can score, i.e. if you win the rally when your opponent is serving you merely *win the rally*.

A game consists of 15 points (or aces), except in ladies' singles, where it consists of 11 points. The winner of a match is the side which scores the best in two out of three games. Where two sides tie near the end of the game, the player who got to the point first can have choice of 'setting' (see Law 7, page 111). Players change courts at the end of each game and the winner serves first in the following game; if a third game is necessary the players change courts halfway through (see Law 8).

Serving should always be to the diagonal court and in *doubles* no player may receive two consecutive services in the same game. Only the receiver may return the shuttle that has just been served, thereafter either player may make the return. Only one attempt is allowed for each service, unless the shuttle is missed.

If the shuttle touches the net either during service or during play this does *not* constitute a 'let' (i.e. an allowed replay) only if the shuttle exceptionally lodges in the net *after* passing over it.

The server must always wait until the receiver is ready and neither is allowed to distract the other by any preliminary feints, etc. Both players must not stand on any lines during service (in doubles the respective partners may stand where they like, provided they do not obstruct their opponents), though they may lean over. If the shuttle falls on the line of the correct service court, as in the rest of the game, it is deemed good.

The 'fault' shot rule

Read Law 14 (h) (page 116) carefully. Under the present rule it is *not* a fault if the shuttle is hit on any part of the racket once (i.e. wood shots are lawful). It is important to realise that a fault can occur even when the shuttle is struck by the wood of the racket and that these shots should not be automatically accepted as good, since they might be hit twice with two strokes or slung.

Remember, however, that when the rule was changed at the I.B.F. annual general meeting in 1963 it was intended to minimise the calling of faults so as to make the game more enjoyable by avoiding breaking up the continuity of rallies. The rule was subsequently changed again at the I.B.F. annual general meeting in July 1968, so that *only* double-hits with two separate strokes or shots where the shuttle is held on the racket (i.e. caught or slung) are faults.

3

Get a grip of your game

The grip

The fundamental of any racket game is a correct grip and this applies particularly to badminton, since there is no other game in which it is so important to have the 'feel' of the object being propelled.

The most important point to realise is that 'grip' should not be taken literally, that is, your hold should be firm, but not a tight grasp. Remember the fencing instructor's metaphor—do not strangle it or let it fly away. Yes, you can treat your racket like a swan.

Check your grip this way:

1. *Forehand*

Hold racket by shaft in non-playing hand with strings facing the floor, handle towards you. Run the palm of your playing hand from the strings flat down the shaft until the heel of the hand touches the handle end; spread the fingers and thumb as if shaking hands (see diagram 1).

DIAGRAM 1

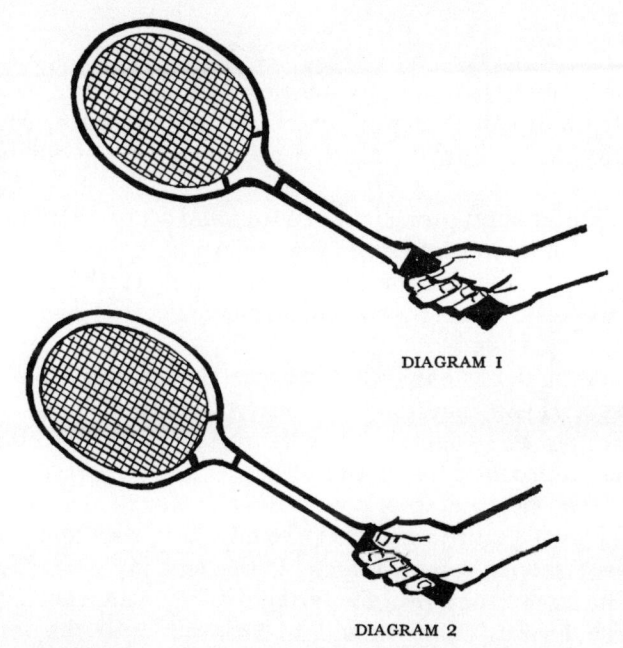

DIAGRAM 2

2. *Backhand*

As above, but turn your hand slightly inwards until your index finger is over the uppermost part of the racket and the thumb is pressing exactly the opposite face (see diagram 2). You will notice that the only difference is the angle of the racket head to your hand.

Some players have the unorthodox 'frying-pan' grip; this is because they have learnt to play without being shown the best way to hold the racket. It can be effective, particularly for attacking net play, but in general it is far too restricting and should be avoided. Never use the 'poker' grip—i.e. with fingers bunched close together.

The wrist

Now that you have a relaxed but firm, orthodox grip and can change it quickly when necessary, you must learn how to hit the shuttle at any required force.

The greatest propellant of power and art of deception in badminton comes from the cocking of the wrist. The amount of cocking will vary according to the speed and power of the shot; even a delicate net shot requires some cocking.

A rigid or tense wrist renders no impetus to the racket head and the beginner will have to practise flicking at imaginary shuttles regularly so that the action becomes automatic.

Test the cocking of your wrist this way:

Play a shot straightening the arm at impact and the wrist should come through at the end involuntarily. The louder the swish, the further back you are cocking. The forward snap should be delayed until the last possible moment and the wrist will naturally come into a straight line with the arm and the racket at impact.

Body weight

Putting plenty of beef behind your shot does not merely depend upon sheer physical strength. To start with, you should never slump back on to your heels, but always stand relaxed on the balls of your feet, knees slightly bent, with your body weight evenly balanced waiting for the return.

Before hitting a shot on the forehand you should turn your left shoulder towards the net, put your weight on to your back (right) foot and slightly bend your right knee. Just before impact, transfer your weight swiftly but easily on to your left foot, and turn your trunk in a semicircular motion by straightening your knees sharply and snapping the small of your back forward.

When you throw your arm and shoulder up at the shuttle, this transfer of weight should make you follow through correctly, finishing up with your right foot in front.

To play your shots in this way it is essential to give yourself plenty of time and room. In other words, always take the shuttle early and as far in front of you as possible. It follows that being able to cover the court quickly is of prime importance.

Footwork

Speed of foot alone is not enough. Quick reflexes are needed so that you can start and turn quickly in any direction. As stated before, your stance at base should be relaxed and balanced on the balls of your feet, and where more than one step is required, make the last step the longest, but ensure that the length of step is such that you can reach the shuttle comfortably, hit on balance and recover at once.

It is best to take short paces when you move off and then adjust your feet before the longer 'hitting' step. Nevertheless, you must not go after the shuttle 'like a bull at a gate', as you will finish up by running off the court, into the net or by sitting on the floor.

Just as important is the fact that if you tear around the court your opponent can use your speed by delaying his shot until after you have moved. There is nothing more frustrating than tiring yourself out sprinting in the wrong direction.

Remember, speed is the natural attribute of an athletic body, but footwork is the basis of good stroke production. A good mover on the badminton court never looks rushed or caught off balance.

4

Serve it this way: receive it this way

The service is the most important shot in badminton, since you can score only when serving, and to add to this problem the rules of the game ensure that it must be a defensive shot. See particularly Law 14 (a) (page 115) and *please* observe this rule as the whole idea of the game is to make it as difficult as possible to score points.

Serving above the waist or overhand is a most unfair advantage and produces the same effect on the game as deliberately 'slinging' shots.

Firstly, you should adopt a natural, erect, but relaxed stance fairly near the centre line and about 2 to 3 ft. behind the front service line, with your *left* foot slightly in front. If you feel more comfortable with your right foot forward there is no harm in standing that way, but, as in all other forehand shots, you will have to transfer your body weight from back to front foot.

As you prepare to serve (with the usual forehand grip) remember that you have plenty of time and do not hurry your movements.

We find that the simplest way is to place your racket back, slightly cocking the wrist ready for the forward swing. Hold the shuttle between your thumb and index finger and extend your arm, slightly bent, to a comfortable length in front of you at shoulder height so that you can drop the shuttle about 3 ft. in front and in line with your *right* foot (see illustration facing page 44).

Incidentally, when serving avoid holding the glued part of the shuttle. It will stick to your fingers. Wrap your fingers around the feathers at the top of the shuttle.

Your weight when you start to serve should be on your back foot (and as you deliver the service you should ease your weight smoothly to your front foot).

Now drop the shuttle straight down by merely opening your thumb and index finger, so that it will drop in the same spot every time. As you let the shuttle go, swing the racket head forward with an easy rocking movement and direct the shuttle to the spot intended by using very little wrist movement.

Hit the shuttle about an arm's length away from you, approximately over the front foot, and follow through. Never try to stop the racket at contact.

It is advisable to practise the low service first, as you can then concentrate on controlling all the foregoing movements and guiding the shot. You can worry about the power later.

Remember that for the high singles serve all your actions must be more extreme, that is to say, your feet should be wider apart, your backswing should go back further and your wrist should be cocked back more.

The swing forward of your racket and the transference of your body weight should be faster and more exaggerated, so that the arm comes right through, ending up over your left shoulder (as at the finish of a golf drive).

After the follow-through you should be balanced on the ball of your front foot with the toe of your back foot still on the floor, having pivoted. The 'flick' service should be used sparingly as a variation to surprise your opponent and keep him guessing, and to do this, use the same action as for your short serve, but bring your wrist through quicker at latest possible moment.

If you find you are serving badly it could be due to the following common faults:

1. Failure to let go of the shuttle early enough, resulting in a cramped shot.

2. Hitting too hard or jerking through failure to relax.

3. Slicing due to faulty grip or follow-through.

4. Cocking the shuttle up, caused by allowing the wrist to work (remember this is the only shot in the game where the wrist is not allowed to be flexible).

5. Allowing your head to come up before the stroke has been completed, thereby losing direction and elevation.

6. Hitting the shuttle too low because of a crouching stance.

7. Failure to use a full, relaxed arm action when serving high.

Further details on serving as they apply to the different departments of the game will be found in chapters 6, 7, and 8, but in general the most important point to remember—as with all other shots—is that you must keep your opponent guessing.

No matter how accurate you are, your opponent will be able to 'rush' or at least calmly prepare an attacking reply. Remember, a poor service which wrong-foots the receiver can be more effective. Let your motto be: Variety is the spice of service!

Now cross under the net and imagine you are the receiver. We will deal with singles first. Here the high serve will be used against you in most cases. Your reply will generally depend upon the length of the service (this is enlarged upon in chapters 6, 7 and 8), but you should stand about 5 ft. behind the front service line, relaxed with your weight slightly more on your left (front) foot. To reach the high serve you must use a sideways, skipping movement so as to get under and well behind the shuttle quickly. If the serve is falling over the back line your right (back) foot should be *outside* the court. The low serve will be used to unsettle you or force you to make a certain reply. You should be prepared, therefore, to move in quickly to take the shot early *at tape height*, so as to give yourself time to play a variety of replies.

In doubles, your outlook should be one of 'ferocious aggression' and your intention must be to meet all low services *in front of the short-service line*, but be able to get back quickly enough to hit *any* high serves down with an overhead shot.

Naturally, the distance at which you can stand behind the short-service line depends on your individual reflexes and any particular weakness you have in your shot production, but it is a good idea to start at about 3 ft. and move gradually closer as you gain experience and ability.

As the forehand is usually the strongest wing of attack, your position should favour it, i.e. about 1 ft. from the centre in the right court and 3 ft. in the left court.

Whatever your position, you must take up a crouching stance with your left foot well in front of your right

Roger Mills

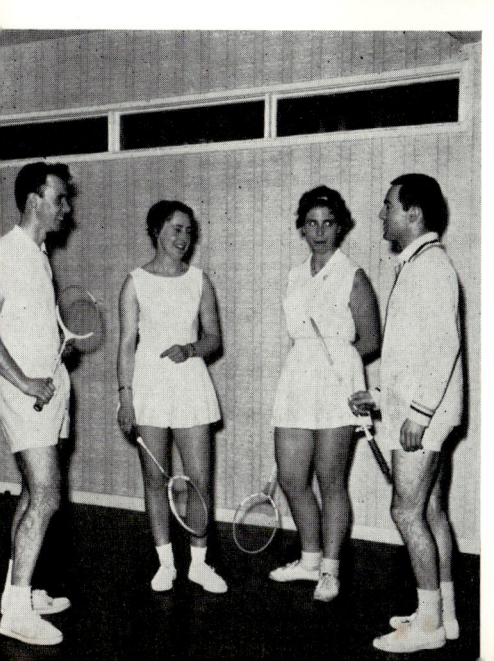

A well-dressed foursome. But there is variety in their attire. Angela Bairstow (Surrey and England) favours a dress, while Ursula Smith (Kent and England) has skirt and blouse. Alan Pears (Hertfordshire) is in short-sleeved shirt, while Roger Mills has a long-sleeved woolly

Preparing for an overhead shot. Note full body weight on right foot.

Just before impact. Note transference of body weight on to front foot and your body partly sideways, facing towards the right sideline (see illustration facing page 44).

Your weight should be evenly balanced on the balls of your feet, with your knees bent, and, just as a sprinter spends hours practising his 'get-set' position from the starting blocks, so you must find the ideal position in which you feel comfortable yet capable of springing like a cat backwards or forwards.

5

Stroke it this way

The four basic strokes and other interesting shots

It is assumed that you have grasped the fundamental principles of footwork, body-weight balance and transference, the grips and shot production, since without realising the importance of learning them, your improvement will be severely restricted.

Now you must add to the 'recipe' of your game (remembering that variety is the spice . . .!) the too-often-forgotten simple 'ingredients' of concentration, timing and keeping your eye on the shuttle.

In this chapter we propose to show you how to play your shots correctly. We have taken into account the differences in size and strength and we feel that these techniques will give the best chance of playing well with fewer errors.

Nevertheless, remember that you can only play as well as you are allowed and that all too often, against a deceptive stroke-player, you will have no time to take the shuttle in the correct (and easiest) manner. At this point, therefore, we would like to emphasise that once you have mastered the art of playing the shots in this way (that is, as they would be coached), you must then try to strengthen your body, and your wrist in particular, so that you have enough power to place the shot where you want to from any position.

The Clear (or Lob)

1. *Overhead—Forehand*

This is the most used stroke in the game and as it is the basis of all overhead shots it is essential to master its execution. As explained before, you must get behind the shuttle and prepare to transfer your weight from back to front foot at impact. Take a good underarm swing, turning your left shoulder towards the net; lean back and throw the racket head at the shuttle (as if you were throwing a ball overhead), wrist leading and your body swinging forward.

Do not hold the racket too tightly, otherwise your wrist will lock and you will lose power, but grip firmly at impact. Try to strike the shuttle just above your head, reaching up as high as possible and hitting with a straight—but not rigid—arm. To clear from the back of the court you must throw your whole body after the shuttle, with your racket following through in the direction you want the shuttle to go. Your weight should automatically transfer to your left foot.

2. *Overhead—Backhand*

With this shot your footwork is of paramount importance, as you must move smoothly from base, ensuring that you have the correct grip (with your thumb up), getting in line with the shuttle and placing your feet almost square to the sideline so that your right shoulder is facing the net and your elbow pointing upwards. You must not turn your back completely to the net as you will not be able to see what your opponent is doing.

You should strike the shuttle overhead with your arm fully extended, having transferred your weight from *left to right foot*, using your body, shoulders, upper arm, forearm and then wrist like a spring uncoiling.

You will lose power if you do not time the shuttle right off the top of the racket. The follow-through is somewhat restricted and the action may be likened to flicking a fly on the ceiling with a towel.

3. *Underhand—Forehand*
This shot should usually be played with the *right* foot forward (unless you are not stretching), with plenty of body weight and backswing into the shot. You will need to have your elbow back so that you can throw the racket at the shuttle, wrist leading, with your body swinging into the intended line of flight.

You must hit at arm's length and flick as if you are whipping a top, keeping your head down. Of course, the exact spot to hit the shuttle depends upon how low the shuttle has fallen.

4. *Underarm—Backhand*
This must *always* be played with the right foot forward and the right shoulder well across so that the trunk is turned with the chest almost facing the left-hand sideline.

You must lead with your elbow and your *racket head* should be about level with your *shoulder* and your wrist cocked and level with your *waist* (see illustration facing page 80).

As a final note, we would remind you that the clear is chiefly a defensive stroke, its main aim being to give you time to regain your position. If you are already in position, however, and balanced, you can employ a low, attacking clear just out of your opponent's reach, though you must, of course, not hit with the same power as your high lob. Whatever type you choose, the all-important feature must be *good length* (i.e. within 6 in. of the back line).

The Smash—Forehand

Fundamentally, the production of this shot is the same as the lob until the point of impact (and you should make the shot look the same in order to keep your opponent guessing). At impact the wrist is snapped down and the shuttle taken slightly more in front of the body and hit in the steepest possible downward direction, passing very close to the net.

Once again it is important to get behind the shuttle to take it as early as possible with a straight arm so as not to lose power. Do not be tempted to jump up and produce your 'killer' from mid-air, as this will make your timing much more difficult and seriously impede the speed of your recovery.

The more severe your smash, the better, because anything of poor length you can put away as an outright winner, collecting valuable points. The threat of a 'big dig'—as it is known by tournament players—will cause your opponent to make other mistakes in his anxiety to avoid giving you a chance to use it, and he will tend to tense up and move further back into the court in 'horrified expectancy'.

More than any other stroke, this shot requires your best footwork, body balance, wrist snap and timing. The higher you take the shot, the steeper the angle, but do not forget that the further back into the court you are forced to make your shot, the flatter your smash must be.

So far, we have emphasised that your 'kill' must have speed, but far more important is the placing, and at this stage we will break it down into three categories:

1. The Full Smash.
2. The Body Smash.
3. The Half-Smash.

The Full Smash should be hit with maximum power at an imaginary line about 18 in. from the sidelines about halfway up the court on either side and should only be used as a winner after a loose shot.

The Body Smash should similarly be used only off loose shots, preferably to surprise your opponent, and should be aimed at his chest and shoulders, depending on his defensive stance. A chest-high smash is always difficult to return, particularly if you are on the move.

The Half-Smash is a somewhat more advanced shot and a very popular method of 'opening up' the court. The preliminary movements are the same, but at impact a slieing action of the racket is used controlled by turning the wrist. The last two fingers act as a rudder, controlling the smooth but sharp down movement of the racket head.

This can be learnt only with practice and experience and you will eventually learn to cut away those last two fingers. This action results in the shuttle being brought down more sharply but causing the pace to be reduced to about half. It is effective even off good-length clears, particularly when angled well away from your opponent.

Although all smashes must be taken as high as possible, you may feel more comfortable striking the shuttle away from your right shoulder, i.e. above your head or even over your left shoulder. To do this you will have to place your left foot further to the left to leave your body and right arm unrestricted. Additionally you may have to do this when you are playing what would otherwise have to be a backhand stroke. This style is called 'round the head' and can be very deceptive, as the direction of the shot is more hidden. Many players develop this stroke until the body arches sideways and backwards to an amazing angle by placing their whole body weight on to their left foot and by swinging their arm with bent elbow and racket back behind the head and round, so that the forearm brushes the top of the head (see illustrations facing page 80). If you become fond of this shot be careful that you are not tempted to hit while off balance.

Backhand Smash

This shot should be used *only exceptionally*, though following on from above, you must hit a shot on the backhand when you would otherwise have to take too many steps to take the shuttle 'round the head'. Reaching to take it early on the backhand will not only save time but speed your recovery to base. The backhand smash can be used to put away loose returns, but will have to be well angled away from your opponent or else he will counter-attack fiercely.

The Drop

This shot must be *stroked* firmly, but your preliminary action must appear to be exactly the same as your other overhead shots; you will then keep your opponent guessing (a basic but essential tactic of the game) and this will be employing deception in its simplest but most effective form.

The technique is to really get the 'feel' of the shuttle and attempt to wrap the strings of the racket around the cork and feathers simultaneously, as if wiping a duster around the headlamp of a car with the palm of your hand, rolling your wrist anti-clockwise.

You should aim the shot to fall as near to the front service line as possible and obviously out of your opponent's reach; the slow 'donkey drop' falling steeply down a few inches from the net can be used to give you time to recover, and the closer to the net, the further up the court you can move with confidence, since your opponent will have to hit along a higher trajectory.

This also applies to underhand, backhand and forehand 'push shots' when the movement of the wrist should be slight so that the shuttle 'dies' at net-cord height.

The overhead backhand drop must be concealed until the last possible moment and, like all other drops, should be 'tight', that is, close to the net.

The great temptations to be avoided with drop shots are:

Preparing to serve. Note cocked wrist

At impact of service. Note body weight on left foot and eye on shuttle

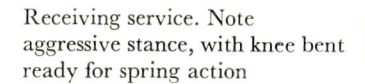

Receiving service. Note aggressive stance, with knee bent ready for spring action

Preparing for backhand shot.
Note elbow

At full stretch at point of
impact. Note body weight
on left foot

1. Making an exaggerated wind-up with over-emphasised power and

2. Forgetting that it has its limitations as a point winner and therefore using it excessively.

In short, play the shot firmly but with finesse; be natural in execution and judicious in employment.

The Drive

If used and played correctly this shot is second only to the smash as a weapon of attack. Unfortunately, most players tend to use it indiscriminately and turn a game (particularly of mixed) into a sort of 'hacking' match. Carrying the rugby metaphor further, you can compare this 'swipe' shot to a fly kick, the penalty being the agony of seeing the return hit the floor on your court several feet away from the end of your outstretched racket!

The drive must be a flat stroke, skimming the net and played preferably down the sidelines unless your opponent(s) is right out of position, in which case you can use the cross-court. To do this you should hit the shuttle about chest height for the backhand or forehand, and the higher you take it, the flatter the trajectory of your shot. It is most important that you meet the shuttle with an outstretched arm so as not to cramp yourself.

On the forehand, before impact, with wrist leading and elbow well back, you must turn your right shoulder towards the backline and swing your body into the intended line of flight, transferring your weight from back to front foot. The further back in the court you hit the shot, the lower you will have to take the shuttle, even as low as knee height. On the backhand you should transfer your weight from the back (left) foot to the front (right) foot, pivoting the trunk so that your chest is facing the left-hand sideline; then follow through as above.

Depending upon your position in the court, you must control the pace of the shot.

It should be used mainly in doubles to sustain your attack, but variety of power and placement is essential, particularly in mixed doubles where the 'half-court drive' is a basic match-winning shot, as its purpose is to make your opponent lift the shuttle from a low-level mid-court. You must learn to hit this shot so that it passes the net player quickly but not hard enough to be counter-driven by the back player.

Finally, the drive can be used as a counter-hit to a smash. You should usually prepare to receive on the backhand rather than the forehand and time your return so that you are moving into the shot at impact. If the smash catches you on the 'wrong side', that is, your unprotected forehand, you can lean back and make a soft placement mid-court return.

Summing up, we should say that the best way to improve your play is to develop and better your shots. This can only be achieved by constant practice with particular perseverence on any weakness. You can never be a complete player without having a competent and full range of shots.

Play it this way—an introduction

The prime purpose of playing any sport is enjoyment, as the more your standard of ability at a game improves, the more you will enjoy yourself. This applies particularly to badminton, where there is a tremendous variety of shots.

Your enjoyment of badminton is further stimulated by the spirit of competition—whatever the level—and in the next three chapters, dealing with singles play, doubles (men's and ladies') and mixed doubles, we are going to tell you how to win—and even become a champion!

The basic aim of this game is to hit the shuttle on to the floor in your opponent's court before he can reach it, but to do this requires a different technique for each of the three events.

6

Singles play

As the court is longer than it is wide, your main consideration must be the exploitation of depth, i.e. good length on your clears, and drop shots close to the net, so that your opponent has to cover the full area of his court (22 ft. × 17 ft.).

Your 'bread-and-butter' service, therefore, should be high and deep, coming down over the baseline; your opponent will then have to hit hard to get his return to the back of your court and there is a high percentage of chance that he will make an error if he tries to hit a winner or too good an attacking shot.

There are, nevertheless, times when you should vary your service to a quick, short one. This may hustle your opponent into making hurried errors, especially at the beginning of a match when he is not fully warmed up. Sometimes after a long rally if he is puffing for breath a flick service just out of his reach will bring you an easy point.

We must emphasise here, however, that normally you must not go for quick points (unless your stamina is suspect, in which case you should either get fit or quit playing singles!).

The basic strategy is to *gradually* gain the initiative by forcing your opponent out of position (that is, as far away as possible from his base, i.e. just a little in front of the centre of the court). This you can do by hitting your shots safely and accurately to within about 1 ft. of the lines; you need not worry about getting too near the sidelines provided your shot is sufficiently deceptive and well placed to make him s-t-r-e-t-c-h to reach it.

In the first set of a match you should never worry if you find that, by playing your shots this way, you cannot seem to penetrate his defence and hit winners.

Firstly you will (even if you do not realise it) be wearing him down—in which case you will hit plenty of winners later on!—and secondly your patience will help you 'get your eye in' and play so accurately that he will become discouraged when you do not give away points.

At the same time this style of play will harden you up and your endurance will improve game by game. We would emphasise at this stage that, much as players do not like to admit it, fitness is 75 per cent of singles. We do not wish to breed a population of stereotyped 'he-man' players (otherwise known in the tournament world as 'runners'), but both to enjoy and win a singles you must work hard at your stamina, coupled with speed. (We have devoted a short chapter later on, giving suggestions for improving fitness, in view of its obvious importance.)

As stated in previous chapters, if you wish to be a champion there is no substitute for shots, but even if your range of ability is restricted you can still be a good player by merely having the strength to keep going. It will amaze you, if at some time you experiment and see how well you can do, if you merely concentrate on getting your opponent's shots back, particularly when you play the return to the point furthest away from where he has just hit the shuttle, e.g. clear to backhand, drop to forehand, clear to backhand, etc.

Naturally, you should not follow this pattern too closely, otherwise your opponent will never be surprised and, although he might run a long way, he will never be outmanœuvred. Your aim must be to discover his weaknesses, either to move one way or the other, or to produce certain shots effectively from certain parts of the court.

You will learn this by varying your sequence of shots to keep him guessing, e.g. clear to forehand, drop to forehand, half-smash to backhand, clear to backhand, etc.

Remember that your opponent, like yourself, must always return to base as quickly as possible, so that it is often advantageous to hit two or three shots to the same place.

At this point we would remind you that the Danish international, Knud Aage Nielsen, who won the All-England singles in 1964, was on two occasions during the tournament well down in the second set, having lost the first, to world-class opposition, but such was his accuracy and fitness that he completely overhauled them.

The Malayan student Eddy Choong was unbeaten in the world for many years mainly because his speed and stamina wore down more talented players.

The current All-England champion and, in our opinion, the greatest singles exponent of all time, Denmark's 'Iron Man' Erland Kops, has got to the top by developing his physical strength so that he can hit the shuttle hard from any part of the court and can go on doing just that for three sets.

Returning again to basic tactics, as the backhand is weaker than the forehand you will find that many players try to protect this wing and therefore leave the forehand unguarded. A fast clear or a half-smash down the forehand side is very often an outright winner.

In general, whenever in trouble you should play a high clear to allow yourself time to recover, but when you are well placed your lobs should be fast and flat, that is, just high enough to clear your opponent's outstretched racket. As we have said before, every endeavour should be made to return to base after making shots, but care should be taken not to be caught 'wrong-footed', that is to say, movement should be checked as the opponent makes his shot.

So often one sees a player, pushed to the back of the court, come 'haring' into the net as his opponent shapes to play a net return, only to have to 'break his back' trying to reach a deceptive attacking clear.

You must remember that the location of your own 'base' depends upon possible angles of return and therefore changes slightly according to the point to which you direct the shuttle into your opponent's court, and your knowledge as to which part of your own court you will have the most difficulty in returning his shot, e.g. see diagram 3 on page 53.

Your drop shots should be as close to the net as possible as (i) this will make your opponent lunge, putting more strain on his muscles and not allowing him to play a controlled return and (ii) you will be

o = Opponent hitting shot.

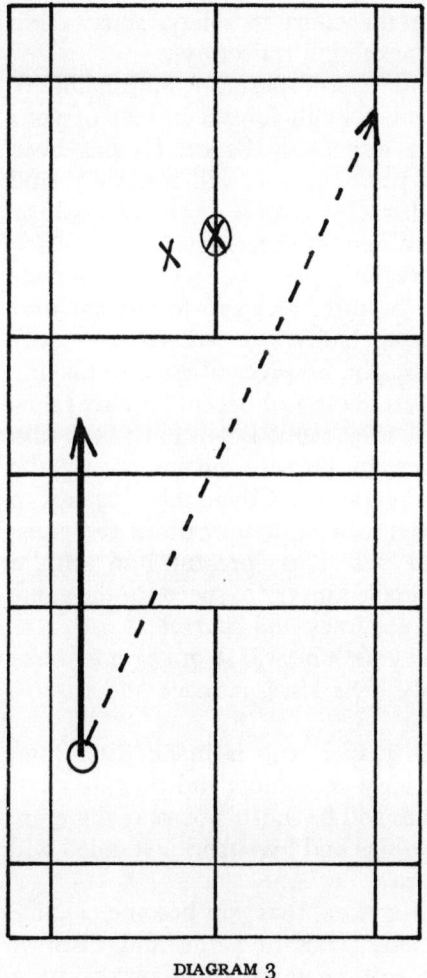

ⓧ = Normal base.

x = Ideal base to narrow angle of the shot which will have to travel the shortest distance.

↑ = Actual shot, which would be the most difficult to reach in time.

↑
|
|
|
Possible shot which could be difficult to return but which would allow time to get back to reach it.

DIAGRAM 3

able to advance up the court in safety, since a lob return will have to be of high trajectory.

You should use your smash sparingly, and mainly to finish off a rally, but enough for the threat of your 'kill' to worry your opponent. Unless he has been manœuvred out of position, you will generally find that a straight smash rather than a cross-court will be more effective in finishing off short returns.

More advanced tactics, such as learning to pace yourself for the two or three sets and to change your game if you are losing badly, you will acquire only with experience. Basically, however, if you are playing someone who has more shots and deception but is slow about the court and lacks stamina, you must keep him moving from corner to corner, cutting down the advantage of his experience. Conversely, against a young, powerful hitter you must slow down the game with high lobs and net shots; present him with a 'lifeless' shuttle and make him try to speed up the game and rely on his own accuracy and control.

If you keep a good length he will soon begin to make mistakes, particularly if he loses patience and tries to smash too much.

When opposing a player who is much fitter than yourself you should vary your shots and play at a fast pace so that the rallies will be short. You may therefore be able to win in two sets and his superior stamina will be of little use to him.

It is imperative, therefore, that you become capable of playing the various types of game and discover quickly which one will be most effective against a particular opponent. There is a saying among tournament players that 'You play as well as you are allowed' and this is very true, since there is nothing more awkward and frustrating than not being allowed to play your natural game.

One last point: Do not give away easy points especially off 'receive' of service. If you want to go for a 'risky' shot, do so on your own service, so that if you make a mistake you will merely lose a rally, but not a point.

Summing up, we would say that the deciding factors in singles are:

1. *Fitness* (footwork and stamina).
2. *Consistency* (patience and accuracy).
3. *Strength* (power and deception).
4. *Determination*.

We wish you good luck in your efforts to obtain these four elusive talents.

7

Doubles (men's and ladies')

Men's doubles always provide the most exciting game to play or watch because of the very fast pace. Perhaps you were fortunate enough to see the 1957 All-England Final between the Choong brothers and Joe Alston and Johnnie Heah, when the Wembley crowd of 8,000 rose to their feet hysterically after a rally of 103 shots.

Your basic strategy must be to gain and then maintain the attack, and to do this a good short service is essential. You should usually serve towards the middle line but vary it at different points along the net, in order to break up your opponent's rhythm, especially if you notice that he has a weakness at receiving a wide serve out to the sidelines. Remember, however, that by doing this you are widening the angle in which your partner will have to take the return. The server should follow in a short service to play the net shots, but stay in a defensive position when serving high (or flicking, see glossary of terms)—following in a 'drive' serve (i.e. driven hard at the receiver) is discretionary, and depends upon the relative difficulty the receiver has in taking it. Important games are won and lost on service and we can give you no sounder advice than to practise it as often as possible.

Just one hint at this stage: Even if you do not intend to serve high regularly during a particular game, a very high one coming down perpendicularly can often unsettle an opponent, particularly if he has previously been 'hot' on receiving the short one.

The most important factor in doubles is the combination of the two partners: Such must be the understanding between partners, if they wish to play first-class doubles, that they are thinking the same ideas and are ready to cover each other's weaknesses or incorrect shots. Confidence in each other's ability will not only encourage their play but will allow them more freedom for their own 'private enterprise'—we are not suggesting that you should rush all over the court playing a 'free-lance' game, but a few flashes of imaginative anticipation can often completely overawe the opposition.

In short, get yourself a partner whose style suits your type of game and play together a lot—you will be pleasantly surprised when you find yourself beating better players who are individualists.

As regards formations, except on odd occasions when a 'driving' rally is in progress, the positions of the players should always be as shown on page 59 (diagram 4).

The need to take up an attacking or defending formation should be anticipated and not left until the last possible moment, especially on a flick service to your partner—you should move into the net assuming that he will be playing an attacking shot. If he has to lob in order to recover you will have plenty of time to move back to defend.

When rushing a short service you should stay in at the net for a weak return. It should *never* be necessary to lift the shuttle defensively when receiving; if the serve is too good to be rushed, play a close net shot away from the server or a push shot past him to half-court. When attacking, the net player should 'hunt' the shuttle, i.e. concentrate not only on putting away the short returns, but 'smothering' the cross-court drive.

Remember that the placing of your smash is far more important than sheer speed—the left shoulder is particularly vulnerable, and there is nothing more annoying than trying to return a smash or push shot off the upper part of the body.

If you decide to intersperse your smashes with a drop-shot make sure it is fast and to the centre, as this will often leave the opposition undecided as to which one should take it. On the other hand, when your opponents are returning your smashes to a good length, a deep fast clear, used sparingly, will prevent them from rushing the net in anticipation of your drop-shot. Avoid cross-courting unless your opponents have been worked out of position, as this tends to place your partner at a disadvantage.

When the attack is lost, the player at the net should come out whichever side he feels is easiest, since it will most probably be to him that the next shot will come—it is usually best to attack the moving player rather than the one who has already taken up a prepared position. Remember that the player at the back can see where the net player is going *and it is, therefore, the former's responsibility to move to the unoccupied base*. If, exceptionally, you are unable to get back to base to defend you should take up a crouching stance and move back

Attacking

Defending

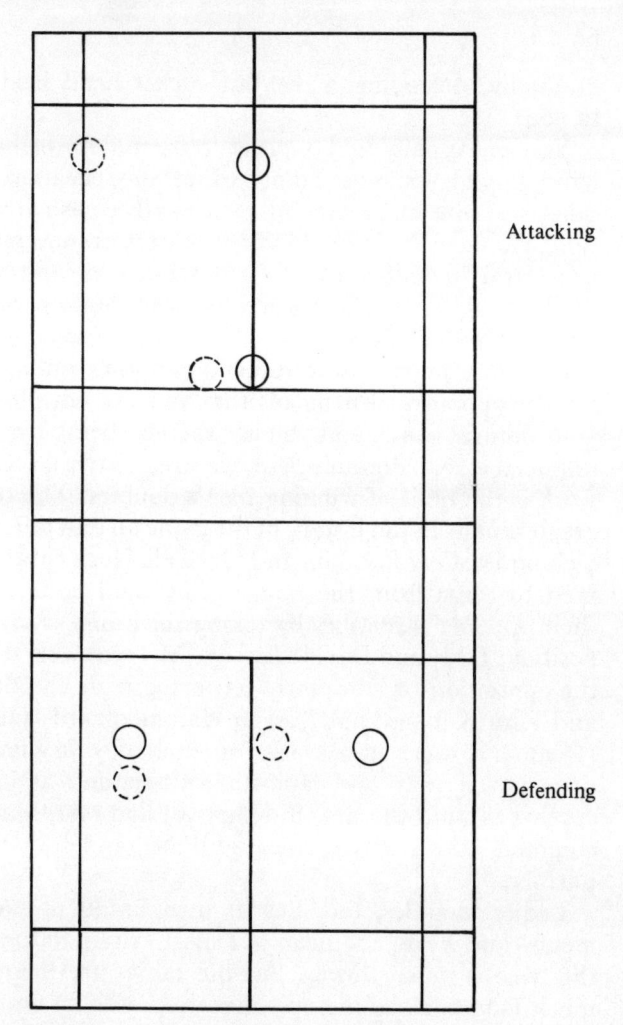

NOTE: Dotted circles indicate different positions while shuttle is being attacked away from the middle of the court

DIAGRAM 4

gradually, defending with your racket head held up to your face.

You will usually find it easier to defend on the backhand, though you must change your stance occasionally, otherwise your opponent will continually smash at your right shoulder. You should vary your return of smashes from straight half-court to fast cross-drives, and even lift high again to the corners to tire your opponent into making mistakes.

One last hint: Never direct your play on to the weaker opponent if it means that you are not playing your natural game, and you are thereby being led into unforced errors. Summing up, we would say that teamwork is the basis of winning men's doubles. The three greatest pairs in the history of the game all had different techniques. Ong Poh Lim and Ooi Teik Hock (Malaya) used to serve from the outside lines and counter-hit their opponents smashes by taking them in a crouched position; Eddy and David Choong (Malaya) wore down the opposition by constantly retrieving high and deep; and Finn Kobbero and Jorgen Hammergaard-Hansen (Denmark) were unbeatable on their day in view of their power play and fantastic anticipation at intercepting around the net. But they all had one thing in common—the ability to always fill the gap left by their partner.

Ladies' doubles, too, has its own brand of excitement—and we do not mean just short skirts! Naturally, the pace is much slower, but the rallies are therefore much longer, since the openings are made by gradual outmanœuvring with lobs and drops. All the same tactics as in men's doubles apply. Low serving is not quite so important, since the fairer sex are not able to stand so far up to the line to receive service. High and flick serving can also be very useful, particularly for forcing a weak lady to the back.

Basically, there are three effective systems which have been used by the three All-England champions from 1953 to 1965: the English couple Cooley-White (now Mrs Rogers and Mrs Timperley) used a mixed formation, as they were better at the back and at the net respectively; the American Devlin sisters (now Mrs Hashman and Mrs Peard) adopted a 'sides' technique even while serving, as this was awkward to play against and one of them was left-handed; the 1964-5 champions, the Danish Rasmussen sisters (now Mrs Strand and Mrs Jorgensen), are agile, versatile and powerful and they use a more orthodox but attacking system. All three pairs have a complete understanding of each other's play and limitations.

Many spectators and male players often scoff at the prospect of watching ladies' doubles, but they are under a complete misapprehension, because a good-standard match would provide them with much food for thought on their own failure to use tactics.

So carry on, girls, you are not just a pretty face!

8

Mixed doubles

To attain a good standard at this event is the ultimate aim of every badminton enthusiast, since both sexes enjoy trying to prove their relative superiority. Unlike tennis, this event is taken very seriously (particularly in England), but at all levels of play it is essential to maintain a meticulous courtesy towards the ladies on the court and to have a sense of humour, since it is in this event that the majority of 'light-hearted' incidents take place. On the tactical side, the back-and-front formation is generally adopted these days, since the prime object is to secure and maintain the attack. In the majority of cases the lady will be much weaker than the man and will cover the net while her partner covers the back. It is essential that the lady have a consistently accurate low service, as this will cause the opposing lady to play a somewhat defensive return and the opposing man will have to go for 'all or nothing' each time he receives, which will pull him out of position on most occasions.

Cross the net for the moment, however, and imagine that you are the opposing man. If you know your opponent's lady is nervous about her service make it a point of trying to 'murder' the first couple of serves—even if you hit your shot out or into the net it is doubtful whether she will be able to serve low to you for the rest of the game.

Generally, you should use the high or flicked service against the lady only, so as to push her to the back of the court, out of position. If used against your own lady she should play her smashed or dropped return (or even a good high clear to the opposing man's backhand) and run straight into the net *without attempting* to 'gather' any high return on the way.

Most of the time, the opposition will adopt the same back-and-front formation, and as they, too, will be seeking the attack, the shuttle will rarely be lifted voluntarily. The vulnerable point in the formation lies between the two players at half-court, and it follows, therefore, that openings must be sought by playing flat drives to half-court and to the back line so as to manoeuvre the opponents out of position and force them to put the shuttle up for the 'kill'.

Teamwork here is just as much the key to success as in normal doubles—both should have the ability to finish off the rally by seizing the opportunities their partner has created for them.

The lady at the net should play only those shots she can control, which will, generally speaking, be those she is able to play in front of her. It is imperative that she should not only put away the short returns but also guard the crossed driven return to her partner's smash *and* intercept, wherever possible, the opposing man's cross-court smash (see diagram 5, page 65).

There is nothing more frustrating than to get your opponent well out of position only to see your cross-court 'winner' cut off by the lady who hits the real winner straight down the line. Nevertheless, she must be careful not to 'poach' for any hard-hit shot unless it is struck from deep in the opponent's court.

In any case, the man should never attempt to drive cross-court until the opposition has been worked out of position and he can play his drive downwards. If you find yourself up against a lady who is 'having a field day' with your cross-courts, play plenty of deceptive straight fast drop shots, as this will draw the opposing man up to the net. As the man can see his partner's moves, it is for her to decide whether she can play and control the half-court shot, which means the man must 'shadow' her and take any shot she leaves.

Now and again you will come up against a 'sides' pair and unless you have worked out a careful plan of campaign you will almost certainly lose, if they are experienced. Basically, the best tactic to use is to play only to the weaker of the opponents, which is usually the lady. You should try to retain the attack the whole time—which should be easy, as the 'sides' pair will have to hit up—using the fast clear sparingly to keep the opposition from rushing into the net to 'collar' your drop shots.

Possibly the most important shot against this combination is the drop, which should always be directed towards the centre of the court so as to make the opposition hesitate. Never try to drive or force the pace of the game other than by hitting downwards; drives or too many clears just do not pay against a 'sides' pair, because they will be able to maintain their positions and tire you with fast cross-court shots. You should move the opposing lady round the court and then

Ⓢ = striker

Ⓛ = lady should be holding racket up

\\\ = area guarded by her

Ⓜ = man positioned to take the more direct shot

▰ = area out of range of smash

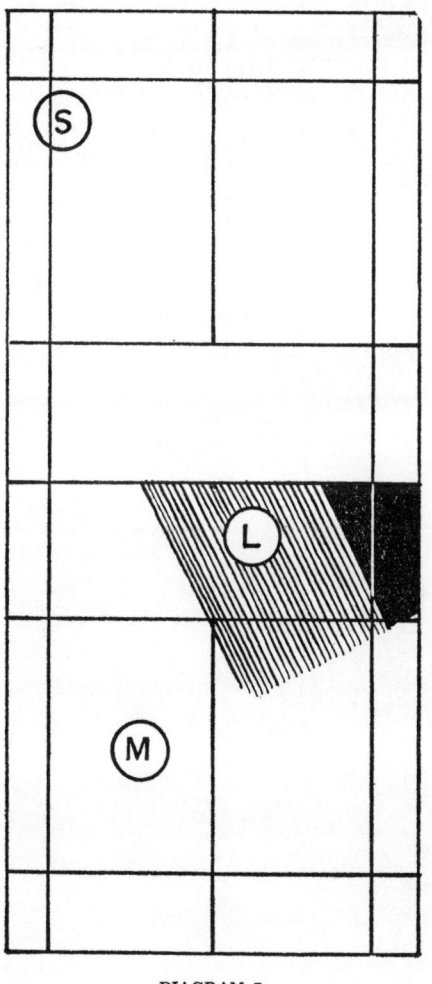

DIAGRAM 5

smash at her body when she is out of position. Your lady should never attempt to play the man on the net, but should play the shot high over his head.

We do not expect to make a Finn Kobbero or a Tony Jordan out of you in this one short chapter, but we hope that the next time you watch a good-class mixed doubles you will understand why there is more 'cat-and-mouse' tactics than sheer 'bashing'.

In conclusion. Ladies: Net play can be exhilarating if you keep your eyes to the front and your racket up. Men: Don't fiddle—kill the 'sitters'. Remember that encouraging and appreciating your lady partner goes a long way.

9

Match play

Skill earns a high ranking in all sport—and not least in badminton. It counts, of course, in match play—and so, too, does determination. Indeed, the determined player can often weigh the balance between victory and defeat. This is so very true in match play where a third-string or second-string pair, following victory over their opposite numbers, take on the better-class pair on the opposition side.

Club matches are generally on a friendly basis before they reach local or county league level. It is as well, at this stage, to show the order of play in the popular mixed doubles, three-pair team matches. They are:

1st round: 1st Home pair plays 1st Visiting pair
              2nd Home pair plays 2nd Visiting pair
              3rd Home pair plays 3rd Visiting pair

2nd round: 2nd Home pair plays 1st Visiting pair
              3rd Home pair plays 2nd Visiting pair
              1st Home pair plays 3rd Visiting pair

3rd round: 3rd Home pair plays 1st Visiting pair
              1st Home pair plays 2nd Visiting pair
              2nd Home pair plays 3rd Visiting pair

To win such a match you would look for your first pair to win their three matches (or only drop one), the second pair to win two and the third to beat the opposition third pair.

Quite often the whole match can rest on the last set between the Home team's second pair and the Visitors' third. And one should never rule out the possibility of the Visitors' third pair pulling it off—especially if they have managed to beat the Home second pair.

You will get your first thrill of competition by playing a fellow club member and then, possibly, will follow local and county league; handicap play, open tournaments, county championships, All-England championships and the international scene.

League matches

You will find these matches have much fiercer competition than friendlies. All teams have the league championships as their target and will fight with all their power to bring glory to the club.

Of course, players will have to learn to face differing conditions. Facilities at some clubs will be much better than at others and it is up to the player to adapt himself.

Leagues may be restricted at local level, but in the large counties, men's, women's and mixed leagues thrive. The mixed leagues are extremely popular and can be relied upon to present many close and exciting matches. One-court halls throughout the country have forced English badminton to produce many mixed doubles 'specialist' players. With the advent of better facilities, it is important to institute more singles in league games.

Handicap play

This type of play can do so much to help the inexperienced player. Six points start in a game helps make up for lack of knowledge and experience and gives the 'rabbit' a chance to adjust his game against a more formidable rival.

Winning and losing need not be so important and this in itself helps the less experienced player to play a more relaxed game. And, of course, top players will so often try to help a player feeling his way in the sport.

We would recommend a spell of handicap play as you are on your way up the badminton ladder. Such play has so much to offer and even more advanced players can get fun and excitement trying to 'overhaul' a large handicap.

Open tournaments

There is no better way of improving your play—and geographical knowledge—than a spell on the 'open trail'. Now you will be really stepping into the 'big time'. Here you must learn to control your nerves in front of spectators, line judges and umpires.

Of course, such competitions can prove expensive—with travel and accommodation to contend with, but if you are in a position to take advantage and play a series of open events then you will benefit tremendously.

Here your mental make-up will be really put to the test in a series of fierce battles, but no doubt you will learn to control your nerves and temper in the rather 'cut-throat' atmosphere of the open tournament.

The tournaments usually take place at weekends and are played on a knock-out basis. The winner usually receives a cup to retain for one year and a voucher which at present varies from £3 to £30 depending on the standard and financial background of the tournament.

The number of 'affiliated' tournaments are quite substantial and are growing all the time. The 1965-6 tournament list showed over fifty open championships in Britain and several hundred 'closed' tourneys.

The 'restricted', 'confined', 'closed', etc., events are only open to competitors of a given nationality, residing in a certain area, belonging to a named league or association, of a particular standard of skill, under or over a specified age, etc.

County Championships

The inter-county championships cover the whole season and provide plenty of exciting badminton. The matches are played in the Far North, North, Midlands and South, with relegation and promotion to divisions of differing standards all helping to add spice to the general scene.

Of course, if the average player has a target it is so often a bid to play for the county team. It can be achieved but only provided your play warrants such an honour and you obtain successful results regularly.

County officials are always on the look-out for talent and once they find it you can rest assured there will be a series of coaching sessions to help boost the lucky individual's standard of play.

Today's inter-county championships attract a very

strong entry and the fight for promotion is extremely tense, with the standard of play generally on the up-grade. If you would like to know more about this whole question then we would advise you to get hold of a Badminton Association of England annual handbook from the Secretary, 81a, High Street, Bromley, Kent.

All-England Championships

This tournament is still regarded as the major international badminton tournament in the world. It is now rated as the unofficial world championship because it attracts all of the world's top players.

The popularity of the championships have increased a thousand-fold since the days when they were first held as a one-day affair at the London Scottish Drill Hall, Buckingham Gate, in 1899.

Crystal Palace, Westminster, Harringay, Empress Hall (Earls Court), and Wembley have all thrilled to the championships. All players agree that these championships have an atmosphere of their own. Every match is timed and competitors know exactly when they will be required to play all through the four days the championships last.

Seven courts are laid out with special court lighting and spectators can revel in such a wealth of world-class talent that very often they are in a dilemma as to which court to watch.

It stands out as a model of efficient administration. A cocktail party the day before and a dinner and dance after the event are arranged to entertain foreign guests. The stadium itself becomes an international meeting place and a reunion for old friends.

At present the events have had to be enlarged to sixty-four in the men's singles; forty-eight in the ladies' singles; thirty-eight pairs in the men's doubles; thirty-two in the ladies' doubles; and forty-eight in the mixed doubles.

Such is the strength of the entry that large qualifying events have to be held a week before and this is a tournament in itself. So great are the entries that recently a number had to be rejected. There is terrific competition to get through three rounds, as this then qualifies a player for the main event (and a free seat!). Such is the high standard of these qualifying rounds that sometimes qualifiers win several games in the main event.

International scene

Every promising player's aim is a place in the men's Thomas Cup or the women's Uber Cup teams. Trips can be made anywhere in Europe according to the draw.

There are three other zones besides the European. They are Asian, American and Australasian. Interzone matches between zone winners are played and the eventual winner challenges the holder of the previous competition.

Apart from the Thomas and Uber Cups, England has regular annual fixtures with Denmark, Sweden, Scotland, Ireland and West Germany. The English Schools Badminton Association, formed in 1960, already holds matches against Scotland and Ireland and will be competing against Scandinavian countries very soon, while the Badminton Association of England is likely to stage junior internationals in the near future.

(Further details are given in the I.B.F. Handbook, available from the Hon. Secretary, 4, Madeira Avenue, **Bromley,** Kent.

10

Watch it this way

Badminton has so much to offer the watcher—especially if he is a budding player.

Much can be learnt about strokes, positional play, footwork and anticipation. Variety in the art of stroke production will also be there for all to see.

It will also help your game if you note how the experienced player who finds himself under pressure produces well-placed clears in order to gain a little time and breathing space. Tactics are important in all sports and this is especially true of badminton.

So often a thinking—but less talented—player can come out on top by the use of shrewd and clever tactics.

As your watching takes in the higher-class game you will become more and more aware of speed and movement, power and stroke variation.

It can also be enjoyable and enlightening to see the way such players appear unhurried and calm even during what are crucial moments. Their great powers of anticipation and keen sense of positional play help to conserve stamina.

With such players it is an education in itself to watch carefully when they are playing a long rally. They go right through the whole range of strokes in a bid to deceive their rival.

On several occasions one player appears in trouble and produces a shot designed to put himself right back on an 'even keel' with the opposition.

Of course, after making such a shot and forcing your rival 'back on his heels' it is fatal to stand still admiring the shot just made. The watcher will be surprised to see the number of players who tend to make such a mistake. Indeed, it is here that anticipation of the return shot plays such an important part.

Having made your shot, you should then be moving into position to take the return. Knowledge and experience in the game, so enhanced by joyful hours of watching, will help you anticipate the kind of shot which should follow.

'Keep your eye on the ball!' is a regular cry in soccer, rugby, cricket and tennis, and so, too, is 'Keep your eye on the feathers!' in badminton.

Naturally, there come moments when, in the act of moving into position, sight of the shuttle is lost—but this should be momentary. Don't get too confident about your ability to pick up the flight of the shuttle at any split second that you want.

Generally speaking, you must keep your eye on the shuttle—especially at the point of impact.

In doubles it is a joy to watch the positional play of an experienced pair. Knowledge of each other's play— the strengths and the weaknesses, too—is a most important factor. It is very nice to see how a pair can boost their weaknesses and 'cash in' on their relative strengths.

One can note quite clearly how each member of the side prepares for any given shot. You, too, can be prepared, having taken in the lessons we have attempted to give in the earlier chapters dealing with shots and the many other differing aspects of play.

As a start, when attempting to broaden your experience of the game by watching, we would suggest you keep your eye on one particular player for a spell. You can see the shot being made and also the whole preparation for the return shot. You can learn so much more this way. Much more, that is, than by just watching the flight of the shuttle.

In order to improve a weakness in your play you will find it particularly rewarding if you go out of your way to watch a player who is extremely talented in the sphere in which you feel you have shortcomings.

You can derive a lot of satisfaction and also help add variety and strength to your own game by watching players especially gifted in some of the many different facets of badminton.

Incidentally, by watching keenly and appreciating the play by applause, one is supporting the game and psychologically encouraging the players.

In this respect it has been proved that audible encouragement is a fillip to better achievement.

An experiment was carried out by a small group of physical education students at Loughborough College a few years ago where they timed each other's stamina at holding up heavy weights.

They were amazed to discover that they could hold on for much longer if the group shouted encouragement just as they were about to 'give in'. (See Chapter 12, 'Keep fit this way'.)

11

Umpiring and Coaching

Part I *The art of umpiring*

The formation of the Badminton Umpires' Association of England in 1953 gave a tremendous boost to the general standard of controlling matches.

Of course, umpiring must be looked upon as an art—especially if you really want to do the job as it should be done.

Senior players have a particularly important part to play here. They can prove so helpful to youngsters during control of a match. He must be able to say, 'I'm in charge', and hold the respect of players. However, one must not adopt a dictatorial attitude towards players. 'Firmness with fairness' should be the umpire's motto. We feel there are no better ways to help you gain knowledge of this all-important sphere than by reading and digesting the following sections on 'Recommendations to Umpires', and 'Hints for Umpires'.

RECOMMENDATIONS TO UMPIRES

(As adopted by the International Badminton Federation)

1. Thoroughly know the Laws of Badminton.
2. The umpire's decision is final on all points of fact; a player may, however, appeal to the referee on a point of law only.
3. The linesman's decision is final on all points of fact on his own line; the umpire cannot overrule him. If a linesman is unsighted the umpire may then give a decision if he can, otherwise a let should be played.
4. Where a service judge is appointed his decision is final on all points of fact in connection with the delivery of the service as set out in 'Service Judge' 27. It shall be the duty of the umpire specially to watch the receiver—see 22 (c).
5. All announcements and calling of the score must be done distinctly and loudly enough to be heard clearly by players and spectators.
   Call promptly and with authority, but if a mistake is made admit it, apologise and correct it.
6. If a decision cannot be given, say so and give a let. *Never* ask spectators, nor be influenced by their remarks.
7. The umpire is responsible for all lines not covered by linesmen.
8. The umpire should control the match firmly, but without being officious. He should keep play flowing without unnecessary interruptions while ensuring that the laws are observed. The game is for the players.

9. When a doubt arises in the mind of the umpire or the service judge as to whether an infringement of the laws has occurred or not, 'Fault' should not be called and the game allowed to proceed.

Before play begins
10. Obtain the score pad from the referee. Enter up the score pad.
11. Check the net for height. See that the posts are on the lines, or that tapes are correctly placed—Laws 2 and 3.
12. Ensure that the linesmen and service judge are correctly placed and know their job—See 'Linesmen' and 'Service Judge'.
13. Ensure that a sufficient quantity of tested shuttles according to Law 4 is readily available for the match, in order to avoid delays during play. If the players cannot agree the umpire should have the shuttles tested, or in a tournament refer to the referee, or in a match the captains or referee. Once shuttles have been found to be acceptable, ensure that they are used unless circumstances alter.

Starting the match
14. Ensure that tossing is correctly carried out, and that the winners and losers exercise correctly their options under Law 6.
15. In the case of doubles, mark on the score pad the names of the players starting in the right-hand service courts. This enables a check to be made at any time to see if the players are in their correct service courts. If during the game the players get

Underarm backhand

'Round the head' shot. The racket is hidden by the player's outstretched arm

Taking shuttle early at net

Attacking a loose drop shot

in their wrong service courts unnoticed, so that they have to stay wrong—Law 12—amend the score pad accordingly.
16. When the players have finished warming-up announce:
    (a) In a tournament:
        1. 'Final or semi-final of . . .' If neither, say nothing.
    (b) In a tournament or match:
        1. Names of players with country, county or club where applicable.
        2. Name of the first server, and, in the case of doubles, of the receiver.
        3. To start the match, call 'Love all, play'.

The match
17. Mark the score pad as the match proceeds.
18. Call the score:
    (a) Always call the server's score first.
    (b) Singles—when a player loses his service call 'Service over', followed by the score in favour of the new server.
    (c) Doubles—at the beginning of a game call the score only, and continue to do so as long as the first player serves. When the right to serve is lost, call 'Service over', followed by the score in favour of the new server. In that and subsequent innings, when the first server loses his right to serve, call the score, followed by 'Second server'. Continue this as long as the second player serves. When a side loses the right to serve, call 'Service over', followed by the score in favour of the new server.

(d) When a side reaches fourteen, or in the case of ladies' singles ten, call on the first occasion only 'Game point' or 'Match point'. If a further game or match point occurs after setting, call it again on the first occasion. 'Game point' or 'Match point' should always immediately follow the server's score where applicable, and precede the receiver's score.

(e) When the shuttle falls outside a line for which the umpire is responsible in the absence of a linesman, call 'Out' before calling the score.

19. See that no unnecessary delay occurs, or that the players do not leave the court without the permission of the umpire—Law 22.

20. If an unavoidable hold-up occurs in a match, record the score, server and the correct service courts of the players on the score pad.

21. If a shuttle or other object not connected with the match in progress invades the court or its environs, 'Let' should be called.

22. Look out for:

(a) Faulty serving if there is no service judge. It is difficult to detect from the chair 'serving above the waist' or 'racket head above the hand'. If there is any doubt, caution the player and ask for a service judge.

(b) The server having both feet on the floor in a stationary position *inside* the service court when the shuttle is struck, and that there is no feint —Law 14 (d) and Interpretation 1. This should be the responsibility of the service judge if available. Where the official responsible considers that there has been a flagrant fault under Law 14 (d), as described in Interpretation 1, he shall fault the server as soon as the service is delivered. However, each case should be judged on its merits and, if it is considered that the server tends to delay too long, the umpire should, either on his own responsibility, or at the request of the service judge, warn the player that he will be faulted should he continue to delay (see also Recommendation 33).

(c) The receiver having both feet on the floor in a stationary position *inside* the service court until the service is delivered, and that he does not move before the shuttle is struck—Laws 14 (c) and 16.

(d) Strokes which are faults under Law 14 (h). These should be immediately called by the umpire as 'Fault'.

(e) On no account allow players to call 'No shot', 'Fault', etc. Warn them if they do, as it may distract their opponents.

(f) Obstruction: for instance, sliding under the net; throwing the racket into the opponent's court; baulking; unsighting an opponent during service. See Laws 14 (d), 14 (j), 16, 20 and Interpretation 2.

(g) Serving and receiving out of turn or in the wrong court. Law 12 should be thoroughly understood.

(h) Striking the shuttle before it crosses the net and hitting the net with racket, person or dress while the shuttle is in play—Laws 14 (f) and 14 (g).

(i) The option of 'setting' being correctly exercised—Law 7. It is the duty of the umpire to ask the player's or players' decision. Announce the decision loudly so that spectators can hear, calling 'Set 2 points' (or 3 or 5 as appropriate), followed by 'Love all' or 'Love all second server', as the case may be.

(j) The players changing ends at the correct score in the third game—Law 8.

(k) A player interfering with the correct speed of a shuttle. The player should be warned, and the shuttle discarded if necessary.

The end of a game

23. Announce: 'Game to . . .' (the name(s) of the player(s) in a tournament or the name of the team represented in the case of a meeting of representative teams), followed by the score and, if appropriate, by 'One game all'.

    In the case of a match in a meeting between two teams always define the contestants by the name of the team represented and not by the names of the actual players.

The end of the match

24. Announce the result and score.
25. Immediately take the completed and signed score pad to the referee in a tournament, or to the captains in a match.

Service judge

26. If only one is appointed he should sit on a low chair by the net post, preferably opposite the umpire, but on the same side as the umpire if circumstances so dictate. If two are appointed, each should sit on a low chair behind the back

boundary line, or in accordance with the direction of the umpire.

27. The service judge, where only one is appointed, or the service judge on the server's side of the court when two are appointed, is responsible for seeing that the server at the moment of striking the shuttle:
    (a) The shaft is pointing in a downward direction so that the whole of the head of the racket can be seen *discernibly* to be below every part of the hand—Law 14 (a). See diagram 6.
    (b) Does not have the shuttle above his waist— Law 14 (a).
    (c) Has some part of both feet in a stationary position on the floor *inside* the service court— Law 16 and Recommendation 32.
    (d) Does not feint—Law 14 (d) and Interpretation 1.

28. If the server does not comply with all of 27 the service judge responsible should immediately call 'Fault' loudly and ensure that the umpire hears him.

    Where two service judges are appointed the one on the receiver's side should be made responsible for calling 'Fault' for infringement of Law 16 on the part of the receiver. He should call 'Fault' loudly and ensure that the umpire hears him. In addition this shall not preclude the umpire also from faulting the server or receiver.

    The umpire may arrange with the service judge, or judges, any extra duties which he wishes either to undertake, provided that the players are so advised.

LAW 14 Delivery of Service

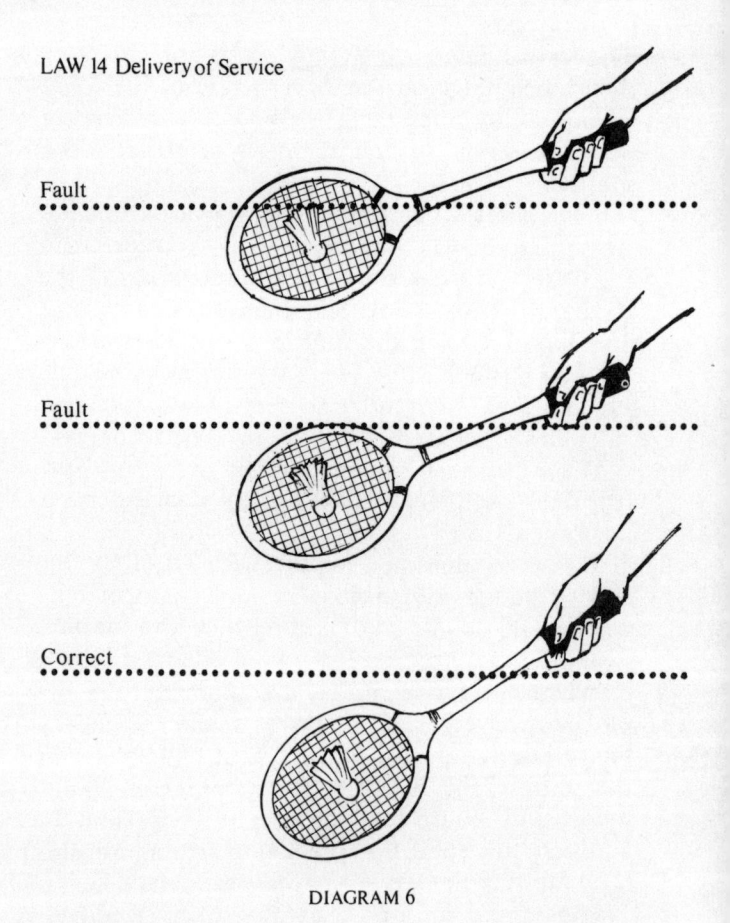

Fault

Fault

Correct

DIAGRAM 6

Linesman

29. A linesman is entirely responsible for his line. If the shuttle falls out, no matter how far, call 'Out' promptly in a clear voice loud enough to be heard by the players and the spectators, and at the same time signal by extending both arms horizontally so that the umpire can see clearly. If the shuttle falls in, say nothing. If unsighted, inform the umpire immediately.
30. Linesmen should be sited on chairs in prolongation of their lines, at the ends of the court and at the side opposite to the umpire.
31. If three linesmen are available two should take a back boundary line and (in doubles) long service line each, the third the sideline furthest from the umpire.

    If further linesmen are available they should be used according to the umpire's preference.

Interpretations

32. It is not a fault under Law 16 if either the server or the receiver raises any part of both feet, provided that some part of both feet does maintain contact with the same part of the surface of the court.
33. It is not a fault under Law 16 if the server, having taken up his position to serve, should then take one step forward before striking the shuttle, always provided that he had not started to swing his racket, either backwards or forwards, before taking such step.

(If you are interested in becoming an umpire, apply to the Badminton Umpires' Association of England. Hon. Secretary, Mr F. E. Hinchcliff, 1, Nelson Road, New Malden, Surrey.)

HINTS FOR UMPIRES

Approved by the Badminton Umpires Association of England.

1. *Before the match*
Ascertain whether any obstructions over the court are to be regarded as 'lets'. Ensure that you know the correct pronunciation of any foreign or unusual names of players, and the identity of the players. Arrange with the service judge or judges any extra duties you wish them to undertake. One suggestion is that the service judge should watch the net to ensure that no player touches it with racket or clothing during a rally.

2. *Uniformity*
It is considered that uniformity in the method of calling the score is essential. If each umpire uses a different method it can be confusing to both players and spectators. Calls should therefore be made strictly in accordance with 'Recommendations to Umpires'.

3. *Calling the score*
It is important that calling should be loud and distinct. One does not want to be a sergeant-major, but the calling should be made in a loud clear voice so that players and all spectators can hear. It seems to be a failing of some umpires and many linesmen that they are afraid of their own voices, and merely say what they have to instead of announcing. Announce the score to everyone and do not mumble it to the nearest players or downwards to your score pad.

4. *Concentration*

Concentration during the match is essential, otherwise it is only too easy to get the score wrong or let the players get in the wrong court in doubles. Sometimes one sees an umpire get the score wrong not once but several times during a match. Anyone can make a mistake, but a good umpire will recover himself immediately, correct it and will not make any more. It is not only a question of concentration and continually checking to ensure that you have not called the score wrong or let a player serve out of turn, but also of not letting a mistake worry you. It is particularly easy to lose a score and forget which side is serving after a very long rally when the scores are nearly level. One method that is found useful is always to keep one's pencil pointing in the direction of the serving side.

5. *Control*

Although the umpire should not act as a dictator or feel that he is more important than the players, it is essential that he should have control of the game. A game can get out of hand only too easily if the players are not used to playing to umpires and start automatically calling their own faults, for this then spreads to other players on the court. However, should a player call a fault instinctively, accept his gesture, thank him, but inform him quietly that you will call all faults in future.

6. *Faults—Law 14 (h)*

Although wood shots are now lawful, it must be remembered that it is still a fault if the shuttle is 'carried' or slung, or if the shuttle is hit two or more times with separate strokes. It is important to realise that these faults can also occur when the shuttle is struck by the wood of the racket. Care must be taken to ensure that a 'wood' shot is not automatically accepted as good.

7. *Service judge*

The service judge should watch the server for foot faults, that the shuttle is not struck above the waist and to see that the whole of the head of the racket is discernibly below the whole of the hand. The contravention of this last part of Law 14 (a) is the most common fault, and that it should be realised that the racket has normally to be pointing downwards at an angle of approximately 35 degrees for the service to be correct. To be in a good position to watch this, it is essential to sit well down in the chair, so that the eyes are on a level with the shuttle when struck.

8. *Service*

When there is a service judge the umpire should watch the receiver for any movement of the feet. It is sometimes found best not to watch the receiver directly, but to concentrate on a spot just on the receiver's side of the net. From there you will probably be able to see any movement by the receiver and at the same time see the service out of the corner of the eye. This will enable you to judge the moment of impact and also call 'Fault' under Law 14 (h).

9. *Movement by server*

There has been some discussion regarding Law 16 and movement by the server before the delivery of service. Some players take up a preliminary position until the receiver is ready, then take a step forward before delivering the service. It is considered that this is perfectly permissible on condition that the server has not started his swing, either backwards or forwards, before taking up his final stance. Should he, however, start his swing either before or during the step forward then it would be a fault. Each case, however, would have to be judged on its merits.

Part II *The art of coaching*

The coach has a really important part to play in the development of the game and in improving the general standard of play. The way he goes about his task can have a tremendous bearing on the whole future of the budding player.

A positive approach to his task cannot only help the pupil to a better standard of play. It can also give the youngest an opportunity to grasp the fundamentals of the game. It can, too, help him understand the laws so much more fully—and that in itself will make the umpire's job so much easier.

What attributes should the ideal coach possess? For the answer we turn to *Notes for Badminton Coaches*, published by the Badminton Association of England.

The Coach

The ideal coach will possess the following attributes:

(a) The knowledge to impart and the ability to do so concisely and enthusiastically.

(b) The experience of having played to a good average standard, preferably at least at Minor County level.

(c) The art of demonstrating each stroke correctly.

(d) The ability to analyse faults.

(e) The ability to place the shuttle with accuracy.

(f) The gift of logically explaining tactics and discussing them simply.

(g) Complete knowledge of the Laws of Badminton.

(h) An approachable nature and a sense of humour.

(i) Infinite patience.

(j) Clean and tidy appearance.

A confident coach inspires the confidence which is essential to produce results, but a coach can only be confident if thoroughly conversant with the subject.

It will be helpful to remember always: that all strokes are entirely natural easy actions with the footwork necessary to enable the weight of the body to be used to the full and to maintain perfect balance; that there is no mystery about tactics for every problem can be argued to a logical conclusion.

Great care is needed in 'correcting' an unorthodox player. Coaches should be flexible in outlook and decide quickly whether the unorthodox player is fully effective without suffering physical strain.

The coach, however, cannot afford to be unorthodox and 'pet theories' and 'favourite shots' should be avoided at all costs. Coaching too many players at a time should be avoided and care should be taken not to dampen enthusiasm by too frequent correction.

Much sound reasoning has gone into the foregoing, but what of coaching organisation?

The system in England is very efficient:

Coaching for the 'beginner' is a club responsibility. If clubs feel they would benefit by instruction in how to coach beginners, County Associations can organise suitable county courses. National courses for county nominees who wish to become coaches are arranged by the B.A. of E. Coaching Committee. Examinations for grading coaches are held each season in different parts of the country, and successful candidates are awarded certificates as county, advanced club or club coaches.

We feel it is vitally important to make it easier for players to start in the game. Facilities are comparatively poor throughout the world and a complete novice is never welcomed and seldom accepted in a club.

The game can be learnt at clubs, but it is difficult unless there is a beginners' section. Coaching centres are the best venues, therefore, and these cannot be organised without the help of numbers of trained coaches.

We feel that by extensive organised coaching schemes badminton could mushroom into one of the world's most popular 'playing' sports. Indeed 'squad' coaching at all standards (including international players) is now a recognised method.

(If you are interested in any sphere of coaching, we advise you to contact the Coaching Secretary, 81a, High Street, Bromley, Kent.)

12

Keep fit this way

Badminton is one of the fastest and most strenuous games that can be played. Singles is particularly exhausting, not only because of the amount of court space that has to be covered in a split second, but also because shots have to be taken low and high at full stretch. It is this never-ending use of your stomach muscles, the running directly backwards—twice as hard as running forwards—and the constantly needed changes in direction of movement that cause your body to 'scream' for a rest, while Law 22 states that 'play shall be continuous'.

It is no use whatever having all the strokes but not the stamina to continue playing them. A hard singles can last for an hour or so and to 'live' on the court for that length of time you must have practised enough and for lengthy spells to have developed the necessary muscles and have subjected them regularly to the maximum strain required.

We therefore advocate playing as much as possible; since the type of physical exertion brought about by the the game is somewhat unique, the best way to get fit for badminton is to play badminton. Be careful, however, not to force yourself to play when you do not feel like it, as this will only make you 'stale'. (Remember that 'staleness' is a state of mind, *not* of body.)

Owing to lack of time and facilities it is very often not possible to play as much as you would want or need to in order to keep fit. If this is the case we would advise you to carry out the following circuit of exercises vigorously for about ten minutes each evening, having acquired a couple of weights (such as flat irons, etc.) of about 7 lb.–10 lb.

Arms and shoulders

(i) Hold weights down by the sides of your legs, while standing up with legs wide apart, and lift weights in a circular movement over your head until they touch, keeping your arms straight, then down again—keep repeating as fast as possible.

(ii) Hold weights at shoulder height with elbows pointing towards the floor and fists pointing upwards, again standing up with legs apart, and jerk arms up as far as they will go and down again—keep repeating as fast as possible.

(iii) Hold weights out (in front of you at waist height) with palms upwards and elbows tucked into your sides, this time standing with feet together and back stiff. Now, slowly drop your hands down to your sides, keeping your palms facing ahead, and then 'curl' the weights slowly up to your shoulders without moving your elbows, and then down again—keep repeating as *slowly* as possible.

(iv) Press-ups: Keeping your body stiff and pointing your fingers as far inwards as possible as this will severely exercise the muscles at the back of your upper arms—repeat quickly but do not 'overdo' this exercise as it is somewhat restricting across the chest.

Stomach

(i) Lie down on your back and with your hands on your thighs *slowly* raise alternate legs to about 3–6 in. off the floor and slowly down, then both legs together—repeat slowly.

(ii) Lie down on your back with your arms stretched out over your head behind you (holding a weight in your hands if you are strong!), pull up and touch your toes and back again—repeat quickly.

(iii) Sit on the floor with legs straight out towards the sides of your body as far as they will go, now touch the toes of your left and right foot alternatively—repeat quickly.

Legs

(i) Standing, rise on to your toes as high as possible and down again; do this in quick succession, leaning slightly forward so that your heels hardly touch as you come down—repeat quickly.

(ii) Stepping on to a chair, bed, bench, etc., with alternate legs—faster!

(iii) Keeping your heels on the ground, bend knees down into the half-squat position with arms folded in front of you and up again—repeat as fast as possible without losing your balance.

An English Thomas Cup team at Amager Badminton Club, Copenhagen. Standing (left to right): Bill Havers, Colin Beacom, Hugh Findlay, John Havers. Sitting: Tony Jordan, Ron Lockwood (non-playing captain), Roger Mills

Exhibition match at opening of Crystal Palace in May 1964. A mixed doubles showing back and front formation on both sides

The England team which toured South Africa, Rhodesia, Zambia and South-West Africa in 1965. In the picture, taken at Salisbury, Rhodesia, are (left to right) Tony Jordan (captain), Jennifer Horton, Ursula Smith, Angela Bairstow, Roger Mills and Colin Beacom

Surrey first team 1965. County champions for the ninth time
Back row (from left): Colin Beacom, Roger Mills, Claude Darnell, Keith Andrews, Rodney Southwell
Middle row: Iris Rogers, Jennifer Horton, Dorothy Hinchcliff (match secretary), Julie Charles
Front row: Angela Bairstow, Patricia Havers

Wrists

(i) Lift and swing (with wrists only) a heavy object such as an Indian club.

(ii) Slowly roll and unroll a heavy object with string.

(iii) Squeeze a piece of rubber or some object with some 'give' (an old squash ball is ideal or a 'sorbo-type' ball).

The length of time or the amount of repetitions that you do depends solely on personal choice (and personal fitness!).

Skipping is good for footwork, provided it is done quickly. If you are a keen 'road man', we advise you strongly not to trudge around the streets for hours, but rather run a couple of miles, sprinting and trotting about fifty yards alternately.

Whatever method of training you use, ensure that you enjoy doing it and do not become bored, because this, like playing in the same frame of mind, will make you 'stale'.

If you cannot do any of the above or have not the inclination to do so, as a last resort (since lazy people need exercise!) we would recommend the practice of isometrics. These are exercises designed for immobile American businessmen. The idea is to hold muscular tension for about seven seconds, performing for about five minutes daily, e.g. press hands hard together; press knees similarly; press knee away whilst grasping it with both hands, etc.

Being fit and feeling healthy will not only add to the pleasure and performance during your game but will also help you to enjoy life and tackle its problems with renewed vigour.

As for your stamina during a tournament, you must plan your schedule. Remember the saying: 'Moderation in all things', and try to be reasonably regular in your eating, sleeping and relaxation habits.

Naturally, during tournaments you will often have to play until all hours of the day and night and may not have time to worry about your diet; then, of course, you may have a party to go to when it is over, and a long journey home the next day, perhaps to play in another match later on. You will become hardened to this, however, after 'doing the circuit' for a season, and provided that you have built up a 'solid base' of fitness you will soon find out that your body can take it.

Finally, a few hints during the game itself: First and foremost, you must learn to relax at every possible opportunity—but without losing your concentration. Tense muscles will not perform efficiently and will speed the effect of the lactic acid building up in your body so that you will tire sooner.

Try to remain composed no matter how badly you are playing and how much you disagree with the umpire, the linesman or your opponent on any decision. We do not expect (and indeed it would be boring to spectators) everyone to play with the Asiatic 'poker face'—so if you do get annoyed don't show it to anyone else but don't 'bottle' it up, either. The only practical thing to do is to look towards the floor and curse yourself vehemently (but quietly!), so that by the time you look up you have forgotten the last point and are ready to concentrate on the next rally.

Remember to pace yourself: Your rate of recovery is all-important, for at no stage in the game, either between points, sets or matches, are you allowed long to rest. So learn to have a 'breather' in between points (without contravening Law 22) and relax between games. During a tournament take plenty of salt with your meals to prevent cramp, and an adequate amount of sugar or sweet foods to replace lost energy.

We wish you good 'pot hunting'!

13

Badminton
a world-wide game—the future

Such is the 'pull of the game that many nations completely unknown to badminton a decade or so ago have developed at such an astronomical pace that they have already produced world-class players.

These countries include West Germany, Thailand, Japan, Indonesia and China. At this stage we would like to stop in time to make mention of what was described in the November 1965 issue of the *Badminton Gazette* (the official organ of the B.A. of E.) as 'the biggest playing landmark which Badminton has ever witnessed'.

We refer to the People's Republic of China's tour of Scandinavia in October 1965, when the members of the Chinese team played twenty-four matches against all the best players of Denmark and did not lose a single one and—apart from one ladies' doubles which went to three games—none of the scores were anything like close.

Prior to this it had been a universally accepted theory that a new nation in the badminton world can only hope to progress through continuous contest with more experienced badminton nations. Though reports from the Far East had told about the tremendous efforts of the People's Republic of China to improve their standard of play in order to gain a position in world-class badminton (as they had already done in table tennis), few experts would probably have expected the Chinese to have achieved this end in so very short a time.

Did not Napoleon himself say back in the eighteenth century: 'Let China sleep, for when she wakes the whole world will tremble.' How, in fact, does a nation teach itself top-class badminton in ten years?

Immediately after the Second World War Denmark and Malaya suddenly and completely swamped all other international opposition. In 1957 Indonesia quietly entered the Thomas Cup competition for the first time and sensationally thrashed Malaya 6—3 in the Challenge Round. How do whole nations improve so quickly and what makes the Asiatic nations so good?

Apart from the natural advantage the Asians have in faster reflexes and more supple bodies, their approach towards the game is more serious, dedicated and scientific than the more carefree Europeans'.

British sportsmen are often criticised for their lack of dedication, while the public and the Press complain that we are just good losers. They forget that we are not state-aided and that it is difficult to find the time or enthusiasm to be dedicated after a hard day's work.

Badminton: The forward view

What of the future? At present the rate of growth of the game is outstripping the size and systems of present administrative bodies. With the ever-widening badminton front, associations must modernise as rapidly as possible and produce development plans. Relatively poor publicity and facilities must be improved if we are to attract young people.

In Britain, in particular, the fact that there is a sad dearth of suitable courts is underlined by our weak standard at men's singles when up against world-class opposition. Had we sufficient courts for singles, we are sure that we would be able to emulate our performances in doubles, for which there is more opportunity to play.

In England the horizon appears to be brightening, however, with the recent formation of the Sports Council, whose main function is to advise the Government on all aspects of sport, including the vital grant-aid. In order to do this four committees have been set up on the potentialities of international sport, increased headquarters administration and coaching development, research and statistics, and improved recreational facilities.

The B.A. of E. will, from now on, be maintaining a close liaison with the Sports Council and, although miracles cannot be expected, as results will inevitably take time to materialise, a few years should see an expansion on the administrative, international, coaching and sports halls side, resulting in improvement all round.

On this latter item, the Minister of Sport has said that facilities already existing must be made available to sporting bodies when they are not required for normal use. It is complete nonsense to shut those belonging to education authorities at 4 p.m. and all weekends and let them lie idle.

It is his intention to provide one first-class facility for each sport in each area. The rest will be just good enough for ordinary use; he has said that social facilities, including a bar, should be included in sports halls, and we would add that comforts for spectators are also essential.

Hard as voluntary organisers work, provision of facilities for those long-suffering martyrs, who sit huddled under blankets enthusiastically spectating until all hours would not only help add to their numbers but encourage them to further support the game financially.

The international scene is broadening gradually; with continued competitions like the Uber and Thomas Cups and more international tournaments and exhibitions, there should be more flexible rules governing professionalism.

At present the B.A. of E. rules state that 'a player shall be an amateur for as long as he receives no pecuniary advantage, directly or indirectly, from playing, teaching, demonstrating or pursuit of the game of Badminton'.

Nevertheless, a full-time teacher can demonstrate the game 'as ancillary to his main duties', and 'an approved national, county, advanced club or club coach so graded at a B.A. of E. National Course' can receive payment for teaching the game, in a part-time capacity only, at classes sponsored by a local education authority' (see Regulations for Amateur Status in B.A. of E. Handbook).

We feel that as the game advances (and, indeed, to help it advance quicker), the rules will have to be modernised to compare with, say, table tennis—where the authorities have said that you are simply 'a player' and left it at that—or else lawn tennis 'shamateurism' will 'corrupt' the badminton courts.

More and more events in badminton are being sponsored by firms and manufacturers and we hope that the continuance of this recent idea will aid the game's growth in many ways.

An English team toured South Africa, Rhodesia, Zambia and South-West Africa in July and August 1965 (Roger Mills, joint author of this book, was a member of the team), and this trip did an enormous amount towards fostering better sporting and social relationships between the countries. Moreover, sport is socially a great 'leveller' and its progress will help to minimise class distinction.

Badminton features in the next Empire and Commonwealth Games in Kingston, Jamaica, and it is to be hoped that Britain will soon be sending badminton representatives to an Olympic Games. We live in an age when sport is an essential part of our existence, a necessary opiate to the daily hustle and bustle.

Help us to convince the world that the best recreational outlet for their feelings is our game, badminton.

Epilogue

The purpose of this book was to encourage you to become a badminton enthusiast, and we sincerely hope that this has been achieved.

Never forget, however, that success is 1 per cent inspiration and 99 per cent perspiration!

Good luck, anyway.

Laws of Badminton

as revised in the year 1939 and adopted by the
International Badminton Federation
subsequently revised up to date

Court

1. (a) The Court shall be laid out as in diagram 7 opposite (except in the case provided for in paragraph (b) of this Law) and to the measurements there shown, and shall be defined by white, black or other distinguishable lines, 1½ in. wide.

In marking the court, the width (1½ in.) of the centre lines shall be equally divided between the right and left service courts; the width (1½ in., each) of the short-service line and the long-service line shall fall within the 13ft. measurement given as the length of the service court; and the width (1½ in., each) of all other boundary lines shall fall within the measurements given.

(b) Where space does not permit of the marking out of a court for doubles, a court may be marked out for singles only as shown in diagram 8 on p. 108. The back boundary lines become also the long-service lines, and the posts, or the strips of material representing them as referred to in Law 2, shall be placed on the sidelines.

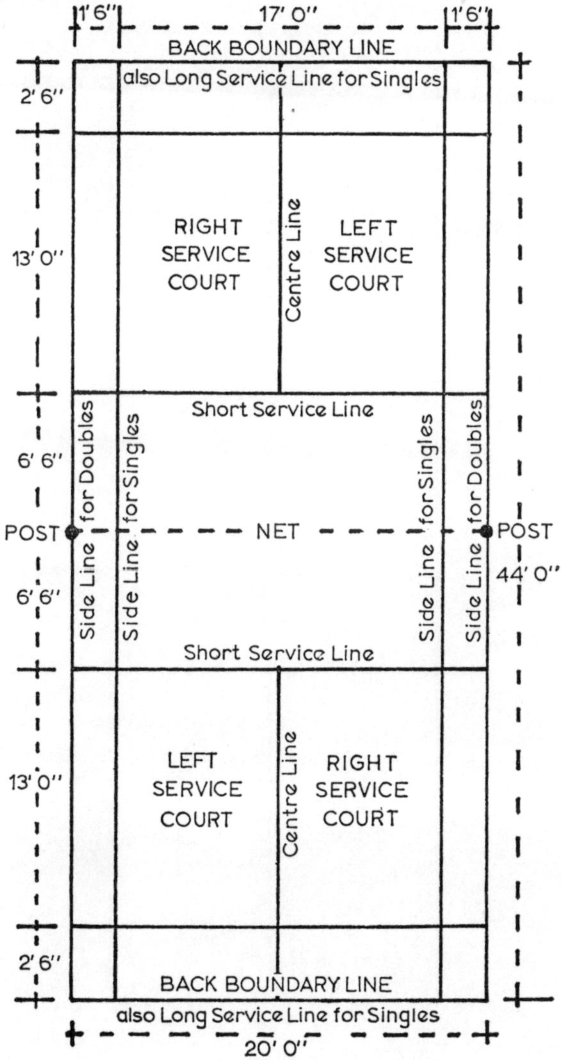

DIAGRAM 7

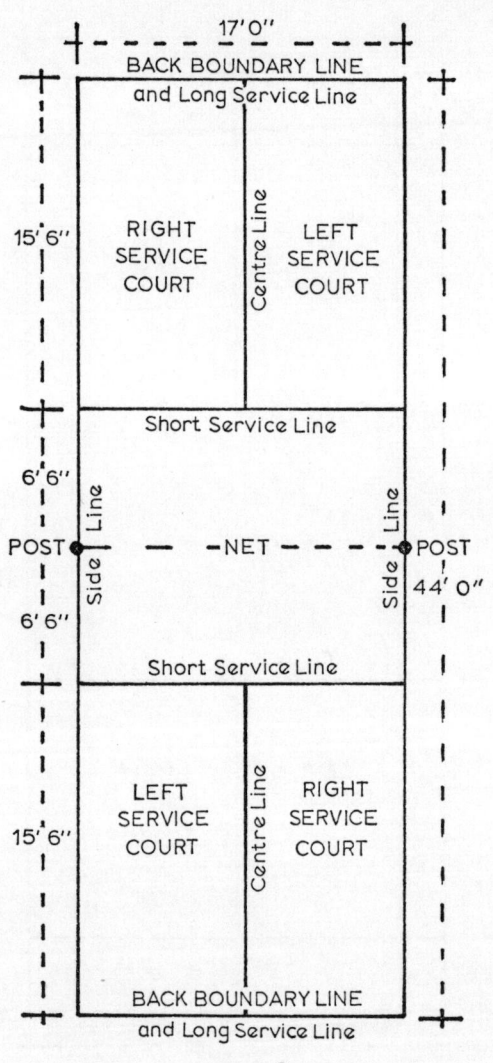

DIAGRAM 8

Posts

2. The posts shall be 5 ft. 1 in. in height from the floor. They shall be sufficiently firm to keep the net strained as provided in Law 3, and shall be placed on the side boundary lines of the court. Where this is not practicable, some method must be employed for indicating the position of the side boundary line where it passes under the net, e.g. by the use of a thin post or strip of material, not less than $1\frac{1}{2}$ in. in width, fixed to the side boundary line and rising vertically to the net cord. Where this is in use on a court marked for doubles it shall be placed on the boundary line of the doubles court irrespective of whether singles or doubles are being played.

Net

3. The net shall be made of fine tanned cord from $\frac{5}{8}$ in. to $\frac{3}{4}$ in. in mesh. It shall be firmly stretched from post to post, and shall be 2 ft. 6 in. in depth. The top of the net shall be 5 ft. in height from the floor at the centre, and 5 ft. 1 in. at the posts, and shall be edged with a 3 in. white tape doubled and supported by a cord or cable run through the tape and strained over and flush with the top of the posts.

Shuttle

4. A shuttle shall weigh from 73 to 85 grains, and shall have from fourteen to sixteen feathers fixed in a cork, 1 in. to $1\frac{1}{8}$ in. in diameter. The feathers shall be from $2\frac{1}{2}$ in. to $2\frac{3}{4}$ in. in length from the tip to the top of the cork base. They shall have from $2\frac{1}{8}$ in. to $2\frac{1}{2}$ in.

spread at the top and shall be firmly fastened with thread or other suitable material.

Subject to there being no substantial variation in the general design, pace, weight and flight of the shuttle, modifications in the above specifications may be made, subject to the approval of the National Organisation concerned:

(a) in places where atmospheric conditions, due either to altitude or climate, make the standard shuttle unsuitable; or

(b) if special circumstances exist which make it otherwise expedient in the interests of the game.

(The Badminton Association of England has approved the use of modified shuttles (e.g. plastic, nylon, etc.) for play in England.)

A shuttle shall be deemed to be of correct pace if, when a player of average strength strikes it with a full underhand stroke from a spot immediately above one back boundary line in a line parallel to the sidelines, and at an upward angle, it falls not less than 1 ft., and not more than 2 ft. 6 in. short of the other back boundary line.

Players

5. (a) The word 'Player' applies to all those taking part in a game.

(b) The game shall be played, in the case of the doubles game, by two players a side, and in the case of the singles game, by one player a side.

(c) The side for the time being having the right to serve shall be called the 'In' side, and the opposing side shall be called the 'Out' side.

The Toss

6. Before commencing play the opposing sides shall toss, and the side winning the toss shall have the option of:

(a) Serving first; or
(b) Not serving first; or
(c) Choosing ends.

The side losing the toss shall then have choice of any alternative remaining.

Scoring

7. (a) The doubles and men's singles game consist of 15 or 21 points, as may be arranged. Provided that in a game of 15 points, when the score is 13-all, the side which first reached 13 has the option of 'Setting' the game to 5, and that when the score is 14-all the side which first reached 14 has the option of 'Setting' the game to 3. After the game has been 'Set' the score is called 'Love All', and the side which first scores 5 or 3 points, according as the game has been 'Set' at 13 or 14-all, wins the game. In either case the claim to 'Set' the game must be made before the next service is delivered after the score has reached 13-all or 14-all. Provided also that in a game of 21 points the same method of scoring be adopted, substituting 19 and 20 for 13 and 14.

(b) The ladies' singles game consists of 11 points. Provided that when the score is '9-all' the player who first reached 9 has the option of 'Setting' the game to 3, and when the score is '10-all' the player who first reached 10 has the option of 'Setting' the game to 2.

(c) A side rejecting the option of 'Setting' at the first opportunity shall not be thereby barred from 'Setting' if a second opportunity arises.

(d) In Handicap games 'Setting' is not permitted.

8. The opposing sides shall contest the best of three games, unless otherwise agreed. The players shall change ends at the commencement of the second game and also of the third game (if any). In the third game the players shall change ends when the leading score reaches:

(a) 8 in a game of 15 points;

(b) 6 in a game of 11 points;

(c) 11 in a game of 21 points;

or, in handicap events, when one of the sides has scored half the total number of points required to win the game (the next highest number being taken in case of fractions). When it has been agreed to play only one game the players shall change ends as provided above for the third game.

If, inadvertently, the players omit to change ends as provided in this Law at the score indicated, the ends shall be changed immediately the mistake is discovered, and the existing score shall stand.

Doubles play

9. (a) It having been decided which side is to have the first service, the player in the right-hand service court of that side commences the game by serving to the player in the service court diagonally opposite. If the latter player returns the shuttle before it touches the ground it is to be returned by one of the 'In' side, and then returned by one of the 'Out' side, and so on, until

a fault is made or the shuttle ceases to be 'In Play' (*vide* paragraph (b)). If a fault is made by the 'In' side, its right to continue serving is lost, as only one player on the side beginning a game is entitled to do so (*vide* Law 11), and the opponent in the right-hand service court then becomes the server; but if the service is not returned, or the fault is made by the 'Out' side, the 'In' side scores a point. The 'In' side players then change from one service court to the other, the service now being from the left-hand service court to the player in the service court diagonally opposite. So long as a side remains 'In' service is delivered alternately from each service court into the one diagonally opposite, the change being made by the 'In' side when, and only when, a point is added to its score.

(b) The first service of a side in each innings shall be made from the right-hand service court. A 'Service' is delivered as soon as the shuttle is struck by the server's racket. The shuttle is thereafter 'In Play' until it touches the ground, or until a fault or 'Let' occurs, or except as provided in Law 19. After the service is delivered, the server and the player served to may take up any position they choose on their side of the net, irrespective of any boundary lines.

10. The player served to may alone receive the service, but should the shuttle touch, or be struck by, his partner the 'In' side scores a point. No player may receive two consecutive services in the same game, except as provided in Law 12.

11. Only one player of the side beginning a game shall be entitled to serve in its first innings. In all subsequent innings each partner shall have the right, and they shall serve consecutively. The side winning a

game shall always serve first in the next game, but either of the winners may serve and either of the losers may receive the service.

12. If a player serves out of turn, or from the wrong service court (owing to a mistake as to the service court from which service is at the time being in order), and his side wins the rally, it shall be a 'Let', provided that such 'Let' be claimed or allowed before the next succeeding service is delivered.

If a player standing in the wrong service court takes the service, and his side wins the rally, it shall be a 'Let', provided that such 'Let' be claimed or allowed before the next succeeding service is delivered.

If in either of the above cases the side at fault loses the rally, the mistake shall stand and the players' positions shall not be corrected during the remainder of that game.

Should a player inadvertently change sides when he should not do so, and the mistake not be discovered until after the next succeeding service has been delivered, the mistake shall stand, and a 'Let' cannot be claimed or allowed, and the players' positions shall not be corrected during the remainder of that game.

Singles Play

13. In Singles Laws 9 and 12 hold good, except that:

(a) The players shall serve from and receive service in their respective right-hand service courts only when the server's score is 0 or an even number of points in the game, the service being delivered from and received in their respective left-hand service courts when the server's score is an odd number of points.

(b) Both players shall change service courts after each point has been scored.

Faults

14. A fault made by a player of the side which is 'In' puts the server out; if made by a player whose side is 'Out', it counts a point to the 'In' side.

It is a fault:

(a) If, in serving, the shuttle at the instant of being struck be higher than the server's waist, or if at the instant of the shuttle being struck the shaft of the racket be not pointing in a downward direction to such an extent that the whole of the head of the racket is discernibly below the whole of the server's hand holding the racket.

(b) If, in serving, the shuttle falls into the wrong service court (i.e. into the one not diagonally opposite to the server), or falls short of the short-service line, or beyond the long-service line, or outside the side boundary lines of the service court into which service is in order.

(c) If the server's feet are not in the service court from which service is at the time being in order, or if the feet of the player receiving the service are not in the service court diagonally opposite until the service is delivered (*vide* Law 16).

(d) If before or during the delivery of the service any player makes preliminary feints or otherwise intentionally baulks his opponent, or if any player deliberately delays serving the shuttle or in getting ready to receive it so as to obtain an unfair advantage.

(e) If, either in service or play, the shuttle falls outside the boundaries of the court, or passes through or under the net, or fails to pass the net, or touches the roof or side walls, or the person or dress of a player. (A shuttle falling on a line shall be deemed to have fallen in the court or service court of which such line is a boundary.)

(f) If the shuttle 'In Play' be struck before it crosses to the striker's side of the net. (The striker may, however, follow the shuttle over the net with his racket in the course of his stroke.)

(g) If, when the shuttle is 'In Play', a player touches the net or its supports with racket, person or dress.

(h) If the shuttle be held on the racket (i.e. caught or slung) during the execution of a stroke; or if the shuttle be hit twice in succession by the same player with two strokes; or if the shuttle be hit by a player and his partner successively.

(i) If, in play, a player strikes the shuttle (unless he thereby makes a good return) or is struck by it, whether he is standing within or outside the boundaries of the court.

(j) If a player obstructs an opponent.

(k) If Law 16 be transgressed.

General

15. The server may not serve till his opponent is ready, but the opponent shall be deemed to be ready if a return of the service be attempted.

16. The server and the player served to must stand

within the limits of their respective courts (as bounded by the short and long service, the centre, and sidelines), and some part of both feet of these players must remain in contact with the ground in a stationary position until the service is delivered. A foot on or touching the line in the case of either the server or the receiver shall be held to be outside his service court (*vide* Law 14 (c)). The respective partners may take up any position, provided they do not unsight or otherwise obstruct an opponent.

17. (a) If, in the course of service or rally, the shuttle touches and passes over the net, the stroke is not invalidated thereby. It is a good return if the shuttle having passed outside either post drops on or within the boundary lines of the opposite court. A 'Let' may be given by the umpire for any unforeseen or accidental hindrance.

(b) If, in service, or during a rally, a shuttle, after passing over the net, is caught in or on the net, it is a 'Let'.

(c) If the receiver is faulted for moving before the service is delivered, or for not being within the correct service court, in accordance with laws 14(c) or 16, and at the same time the server is also faulted for a service infringement, it shall be a 'Let'.

(d) When a 'Let' occurs, the play since the last service shall not count, and the player who served shall serve again except when Law 12 is applicable.

18. If the server, in attempting to serve, misses the shuttle, it is not a fault; but if the shuttle be touched by the racket, a service is thereby delivered.

19. If, when in play, the shuttle strikes the net and remains suspended there, or strikes the net and falls

towards the ground on the striker's side of the net, or hits the ground outside the court and an opponent then touches the net or shuttle with his racket or person, there is no penalty, as the shuttle is not then in play.

20. If a player has a chance of striking the shuttle in a downward direction when quite near the net, his opponent must not put up his racket near the net on the chance of the shuttle rebounding from it. This is obstruction within the meaning of Law 14 (j).

A player may, however, hold up his racket to protect his face from being hit if he does not thereby baulk his opponent.

21. It shall be the duty of the umpire to call 'Fault' or 'Let' should either occur, without appeal being made by the players, and to give his decision on any appeal regarding a point in dispute, if made before the next service; and also to appoint linesmen and service judges at his discretion. The umpire's decision shall be final, but he shall uphold the decision of a linesman or service judge. This shall not preclude the umpire also from faulting the server or receiver. Where, however, a referee is appointed, an appeal shall lie to him from the decision of an umpire on questions of law only.

Continuous Play

22. Play shall be continuous from the first service until the match be concluded; except that (a) in the International Badminton Championship and in the Ladies' International Badminton Championship there shall be allowed an interval not exceeding five minutes between the second and third games of a match; (b) in

countries where climatic conditions render it desirable, there shall be allowed, subject to the previously published approval of the National Organisation concerned, an interval not exceeding five minutes between the second and third games of a match, in singles or doubles, or both; and (c) when necessitated by circumstances not within the control of the players, the umpire may suspend play for such a period as he may consider necessary.

If play be suspended the existing score shall stand and play be resumed from that point. Under no circumstances shall play be suspended to enable a player to recover his strength or wind, or to receive instruction or advice. Except in the case of any interval already provided for above, no player shall be allowed to leave the court until the match be concluded without the umpire's consent. The umpire shall be the sole judge of any suspension of play and he shall have the right to disqualify an offender.

(The Badminton Association of England has not sanctioned any interval between the second and third games of a match except in international matches.)

Interpretations

1. Any movement or conduct by the server that has the effect of breaking the continuity of service after the server and receiver have taken their positions to serve and to receive the service is a preliminary feint. (*Vide* Law 14 (d))

2. It is obstruction if a player invade an opponent's court with racket or person in any degree except as permitted in Law 14 (f).

(*Vide* Law 14 (j))

3. Where necessary on account of the structure of a building, the local Badminton Authority may, subject to the right of veto of its National Organisation, make by-laws dealing with cases in which a shuttle touches an obstruction.

Glossary of terms

ACE (or point)—unit of scoring.
B.A.—Abbreviation for Badminton Association.
BACKHAND—Strokes played with racket arm across body.
BACKSWING—Part of stroke taking racket back to position for forward swing.
BASELINES—Not a rule-book term, but long service lines and boundary of court at both ends.
BIRD—Common term for shuttlecock (or feather).
CLEAR—Stroke sending shuttle high or deep to back of court at other end.
COURT—Area covered by boundary and sidelines.
CROSS-COURT—Stroke placing shuttle diagonally across court.
DOUBLE-HIT—Hitting shuttle twice with same stroke. It is a fault.
DRIVE—Stroke hitting shuttle hard so that flight is horizontal and fast.
DROP SHOT—Stroke from any part of court hit softly so it just clears net and then falls sharply.
FAULT—Violation of playing rules.
FLICK—Quick turn of wrist to increase speed of service and for stroke.
FLIGHT—Path of shuttle through air.
FOLLOW THROUGH—Part of stroke after impact.

FOOT FAULT—Violation of rules when feet of server or receiver are misplaced before impact.

FOREHAND—Strokes played with racket arm on natural side of body.

FORWARD SWING—Part of stroke taking racket forward to point of impact.

FRONT AND BACK—Mixed doubles formation with lady at net and man at back of court.

GAME—Unit of scoring. Usually 15 points in doubles and men's singles and 11 points in women's singles.

GUT—Material for racket strings.

HAIRPIN DROP (or 'donkey')—Drop shot steeply curved up one side of net and straight down the other.

IN AND OUT—A doubles formation.

I.B.F.—International Badminton Federation.

LET—Stoppage of game and re-play of rally (allowed by Laws).

LOB—Another term for a clear.

LOVE ALL—Scoring term denoting both sides at 0.

MATCH—Series of games, the best of three, to determine winner.

NET CORDS—Shots striking top of net before going over.

OVERHEAD—Stroke played above head height.

PASS—To direct shuttle to either side, or out of reach of, an opponent.

POINT—Smallest unit of scoring.

RALLY—Exchange of shots from time shuttle is in play and dead. Rallies are known by number of consecutive strokes.

RECEIVER—Player receiving service.

RETURN—Hit shuttle back over net.

ROUND-AND-ROUND—a doubles system used by weaker

pairs to protect the backhand side by running into on shots hit from the forehand side.

RUBBER—Deciding game or match.

SERVE—Putting shuttle into play.

SERVER—Playing delivering service.

SETTING—Playing of extra points when score is tied at scores laid down for different types of matches.

SIDES—A doubles formation.

SITTER—Shot which appears to hang in air, waiting for the kill.

SLING—Shot held on the racket and scooped over the net. It is a fault.

SMASH—Downward stroke hit with power.

TENNIS ELBOW—Inflammation of tendons in arm.

WOBBLER—Shuttle that does not fly smoothly.

WOOD SHOTS—Shots hit on the frame or handle of racket. At present these are legal.

Recommended reading

World Badminton (bi-monthly—price: 20p) available from the Editor, 4, Madeira Avenue, Bromley, Kent.

The Badminton Gazette (six issues from October to April), available from the Circulation Manager, 12A, Palmerston Road, Buckhurst Hill, Essex (price: 20p)

The Badminton Association of England Handbook, available from the Secretary, 81a, High Street, Bromley, Kent.

The International Badminton Federation Handbook, available from the Hon. Secretary, 4, Madeira Avenue, Bromley, Kent.